PAUL

for

EVERYONE

2 CORINTHIANS

PAUL
for
EVERYONE

2 CORINTHIANS

TOM
WRIGHT

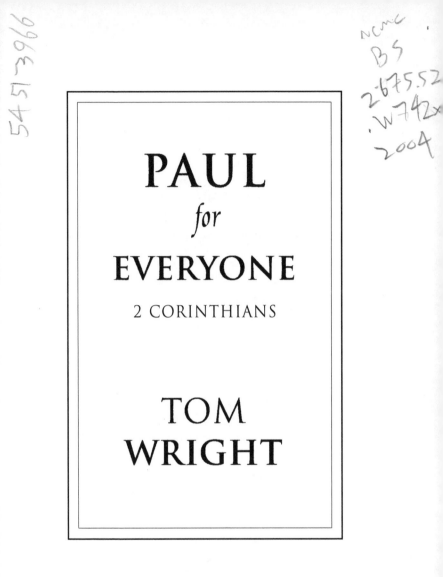

SPCK

Westminster John Knox Press

First published in Great Britain in 2003 by
Society for Promoting Christian Knowledge
Holy Trinity Church
Marylebone Road
London NW1 4DU

This second edition copublished in 2004 by the Society for Promoting
Christian Knowledge, London, and Westminster John Knox Press, 100
Witherspoon Street, Louisville, KY 40202.

04 05 06 07 08 09 10 11 12 13 — 10 9 8 7 6 5 4 3 2

British Library Cataloguing-in-Publication Data
A catalogue record for this book is available from the British Library.

ISBN: 0-281-05306-5 (U.K. edition)

United States Library of Congress Cataloging-in-Publication Data is
on file at the Library of Congress, Washington, D.C.

ISBN: 0-664-22792-9 (U.S. edition)

Typeset by Pioneer Associates, Perthshire
Printed in Great Britain at
Ashford Colour Press

CONTENTS

CONTENTS

INTRODUCTION

On the very first occasion when someone stood up in public to tell people about Jesus, he made it very clear: this message is for *everyone*.

It was a great day – sometimes called the birthday of the church. The great wind of God's spirit had swept through Jesus' followers and filled them with a new joy and a sense of God's presence and power. Their leader, Peter, who only a few weeks before had been crying like a baby because he'd lied and cursed and denied even knowing Jesus, found himself on his feet explaining to a huge crowd that something had happened which had changed the world for ever. What God had done for him, Peter, he was beginning to do for the whole world: new life, forgiveness, new hope and power were opening up like spring flowers after a long winter. A new age had begun in which the living God was going to do new things in the world – beginning then and there with the individuals who were listening to him. 'This promise is for *you*,' he said, 'and for your children, and for everyone who is far away' (Acts 2.39). It wasn't just for the person standing next to you. It was for everyone.

Within a remarkably short time this came true to such an extent that the young movement spread throughout much of the known world. And one way in which the *everyone* promise worked out was through the writings of the early Christian leaders. These short works – mostly letters and stories about Jesus – were widely circulated and eagerly read. They were never intended for either a religious or intellectual elite. From the very beginning they were meant for everyone.

That is as true today as it was then. Of course, it matters that some people give time and care to the historical evidence, the meaning of the original words (the early Christians wrote in Greek), and the exact and particular force of what different writers were saying about God, Jesus, the world and themselves. This series is based quite closely on that sort of work. But the point of it all is that the message can get out to everyone, especially to people who wouldn't normally read a book with footnotes and Greek words in it. That's the sort of person for whom these books are written. And that's why there's a glossary, in the back, of the key words that you can't really get along without, with a simple description of what they mean. Whenever you see a word in **bold type** in the text, you can go to the back and remind yourself what's going on.

There are of course many translations of the New Testament available today. The one I offer here is designed for the same kind of reader: one who mightn't necessarily understand the more formal, sometimes even ponderous, tones of some of the standard ones. I have tried, naturally, to keep as close to the original as I can. But my main aim has been to be sure that the words can speak not just to some people, but to everyone.

Paul's second letter to Corinth is very different from the first one. Something terrible had happened, and we feel his pain from the very opening lines. In this letter he goes down deeper into sorrow and hurt, and what to do about it, than he does anywhere else, and he emerges with a deeper, clearer vision of what it meant that Jesus himself suffered for and with us and rose again in triumph. The letter itself comes through the tragedy and out into the sunlight, and has a lot to teach us as we make that journey from time to time ourselves. So here it is: Paul for everyone – 2 Corinthians!

Tom Wright

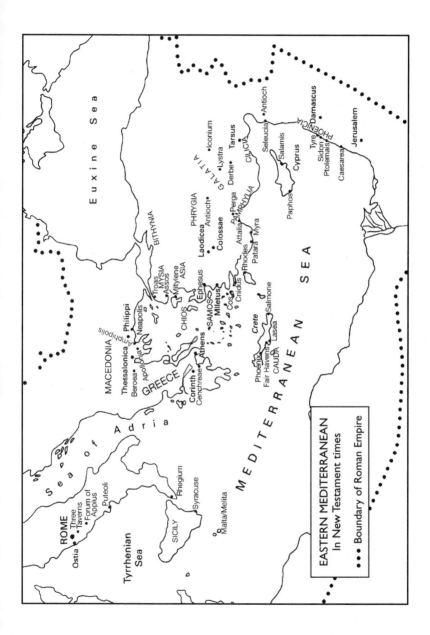

EASTERN MEDITERRANEAN
In New Testament times

• • • • Boundary of Roman Empire

2 CORINTHIANS 1.1–7

The God of All Comfort

¹Paul, an apostle of King Jesus through God's will, and Timothy our brother; to God's assembly in Corinth, with all God's people in the whole of Achaea: ²grace and peace to you from God our father and the Lord, King Jesus!

³Let us bless God, the father of our Lord, King Jesus; he is the father of mercies and the God of all comfort. ⁴He comforts us in all our trouble, so that we can then comfort people in every kind of trouble, through the comfort with which God comforts us. ⁵Just as we have an overflowing share of the Messiah's sufferings, you see, so we have an overflowing share in comfort through the Messiah. ⁶If we are troubled, it's because of your comfort and salvation; if we are comforted, it's because of your comfort, which comes about as you bear patiently with the same sufferings that we are going through. ⁷And our hope about you remains firm, because we know that, just as you've shared in our sufferings, so you will also share in our comfort.

The weekend I began work on this book was the weekend when Queen Elizabeth the Queen Mother died. She had become a unique British institution. She was 101 years old, one of the few people ever to live in three centuries.

The message was flashed around the world in news bulletins. The Queen Mother had been a familiar figure to millions, and had won the affection, admiration and love of people around the world, not least through the comfort she brought to thousands who lost homes, loved ones and livelihoods during the Second World War.

Now it was the turn of her own family to feel the loss, and they felt it keenly. The television showed pictures of them getting together to comfort one another. And the weekend when it all happened was the weekend of Easter. The Queen Mother died on Holy Saturday, the day between Good Friday

1

and Easter Day, the day when the church quietly and sorrow-fully remembers Jesus lying in his tomb. It is an extraordinary moment, poised between sorrow and comfort.

The Queen Mother was known for pithy, and often funny, sayings. But one of her most-quoted lines was from the height of the war. She had made many visits to the East End of London which had suffered most from bomb damage, but finally her own home, Buckingham Palace, was hit by a bomb, causing a good deal of damage. 'At last,' she said, 'I can look the East End in the face.' She had suffered something of what they had suffered, and the comfort she brought them by her continued presence was all the stronger.

Paul's theme throughout this letter is the strange royal comfort that comes through the suffering and death, and the new **resurrection-life**, of Israel's **Messiah**, Jesus, the Lord of the world. This is the letter above all where he explores the meaning of the cross in terms of personal suffering – his own, and that of all the Messiah's people. If in Galatians he is angry, if in Philippians he is joyful, in this letter his deep sorrow, and the raw wounds of his own recent suffering, are very apparent. He is still capable of humour, and some of what he writes here is quite sparkling. But he writes, so to speak, as one who has just emerged from the ruins of his own house after a bombing raid; and he is all the more able to speak of comfort because of what he himself has just gone through.

What has happened? What has caused such intense suffer-ing as to leave a mark not only on his body but, as we shall see, on the very way he writes? How has it affected his relationship with the lively but often muddled church in Corinth? We shall explore all of these as the letter proceeds. But what we have in this opening passage is the lens through which Paul was deter-mined to view all suffering, all the troubles of the world, his own included. It is the lens of the **gospel**; and here the gospel is turned into prayer.

The gospel, as he summarized it in 1 Corinthians 15.3–8, is about Jesus the Messiah: that he 'died for our sins according to the scriptures, that he was buried, and that he was raised on the third day according to the scriptures'. It matters vitally to Paul that these were real events which really took place. But it matters just as much that they become the lens through which the whole world can be seen in proper focus, the grid on which all reality and experience can be plotted. And here, turning his thoughts into prayer, we see what that might mean.

The opening greeting (verses 1–2) follows the pattern which Paul adapted from regular letter-writing in the ancient world. But he filled it, of course, with the particular meanings of the gospel. We notice, to start with, that the circle of readers has widened. In his first letter to Corinth (1 Corinthians 1.2) he simply addressed the Christians in Corinth itself – though reminding them that they were part of a worldwide family. But in the short space of time, perhaps at most a couple of years, between the first letter and this one, the gospel has spread out from Corinth to the other towns and villages of southern Greece, known as 'Achaea'. The very address thus bears witness to the power of the gospel which was still at work. 'All God's people in the whole of Achaea': an increasing number, not many known to Paul personally, but all of them beloved by God, and all of them, sooner or later, in need of the comfort of the gospel.

Paul often begins the main part of his letters with a prayer in which he lays before God the main theme he wants to get across to his readers. There is no problem here in discovering what it is. He repeats the word 'comfort' in one form or another ten times in five verses. To say that this is obviously what's on his mind doesn't put it strongly enough; it sounds almost like an obsession.

Actually, the word he uses is a bit more many-sided than 'comfort'. It can mean 'to call someone to come near', 'to make

3

a strong appeal or exhortation', or 'to treat in an inviting or friendly way'. The whole idea of the word is that one person is being with another, speaking words which change their mood and situation, giving them courage, new hope, new direction, new insights which will alter the way they face the next moment, the next day, the rest of their life. And when you put all that together in a bottle, shake it up, and pour it out for someone who is in the middle of deep suffering, the best word we can come up with to describe the effect is probably 'comfort'. If we said 'console' or 'consolation' that would pick up one aspect of it; but when you 'console' someone you simply bring them back from utter despair to ordinary unhappiness. The word Paul uses here, over and over again, does more than that. It meets people where they are, and brings them right on to the point where they are strong enough to see new hope, new possibilities, new ways forward.

At the heart of this prayer, and of the gospel, is the fact that *what is true of the Messiah becomes true of his people*. This is a central principle for Paul, not simply as a powerful idea and belief but as a fact of experience. The letter returns to this again and again, in what some have called a pattern of 'interchange': the Messiah died, so his people die in him, sharing his sufferings; the Messiah rose again, so his people rise again in him, knowing the power of the resurrection to comfort and heal, already in the present time, and cherishing the hope that one day they will be given new, resurrection bodies like the one the Messiah himself now has. This is basic to a good deal of the letter.

But as well as the interchange between the Messiah and his people we also see, here and throughout the letter, a similar interchange between the **apostle** and the churches to whom he writes. When he suffers, the churches are comforted; when he is comforted, that comfort is passed on to them too. The idea of the isolated individual, living his or her own life in a sealed-off compartment away from the rest of the world, is totally foreign to Paul. Precisely because the gospel is about love, the love of God going out to embrace the world in the Messiah, the love of the apostle going out to the communities 'in the Messiah' that have come into being through his work, this pattern of interchange operates in a thousand different ways. What happens to them, and what happens to Paul himself, are intertwined.

And all is from God himself. Paul's prayer highlights God as 'the father of mercies and the God of all comfort', and throughout the letter Paul emphasizes that God himself is at work in and through the strange and troubling things that are happening. What happens in and through the Messiah, and the gospel, is what God is doing. We should not miss the sense, throughout this letter, that Paul's deep experience of pain and sorrow has led him to a new vision of God. And that vision, shaped by the Messiah, is a vision of light and love. Light enough to see how to move forward from tragedy to glory; love enough to know that one is held in the divine embrace which will not only comfort in the present but remain faithful and victorious into the future.

2 CORINTHIANS 1.8–14

Unbearably Crushed

[8]You see, my dear family, we don't want to keep you in the dark about the suffering we went through in Asia. The load we had to carry was far too heavy for us; it got to the point where we gave up on life itself. [9]Yes: deep inside ourselves we received the death sentence. This was to stop us relying on ourselves, and to make us rely on the God who raises the dead. [10]He rescued us from such a great and deadly peril, and he'll do it again; we have placed our hope in him, that he'll do it again! [11]But you must co-operate with us through prayer for us, so that when

5

God gives us this gift, answering the prayers of so many, all the more will give thanks because of what's happened to us.

[12]This is what we boast of, you see; this is what our conscience is telling us: that our conduct in the world, and in particular in relation to you, has been marked by holiness and godly sincerity, not in merely human wisdom but in God's grace. [13]We are not writing anything to you, after all, except what you can read and understand. And I hope you will go on understanding right through to the end, [14]just as you have understood us already – well, partly, at least! You should regard us as your pride and joy, just as we regard you like that, at the day of our Lord Jesus.

You watch from a distance as a friend walks down the street. You see him turn and go into a house. He strides in cheerfully and purposefully. You wait for a few minutes. Then you see him come out again – only now you see, to your horror, that he is limping, staggering along, with bruises on his face and blood trickling from one arm. You are filled with pity and sympathy, but also with puzzlement: *what on earth happened in that house?*

The historian, particularly the ancient historian, is often in the position of the puzzled spectator. We may have evidence about an early phase of someone's career, and then again a later phase; but what happened in between is often hidden from us. So it is with Paul. He has gone into the house, striding cheerfully along; we have watched him do so in 1 Corinthians. Now we see him emerge again, battered and bruised. Even his style of writing seems to have changed. But we don't know what happened inside.

Nor does he tell us. Like many people in the ancient world, he was more interested in what illness or suffering *meant* than in giving us a detailed account of his symptoms. Most of what we know is in these verses; we can glean a little from things he says later in the letter, but it doesn't amount to much. He simply refers to 'the suffering we went through in Asia' (the Roman province of 'Asia' was roughly the western half of modern Turkey, with Ephesus in the middle of its west coast; Ephesus was where Paul was staying when he wrote 1 Corinthians). What had happened?

Acts doesn't help at this point, either. Perhaps, if Paul was imprisoned and ill-treated in Ephesus – as seems likely – the author of Acts was anxious not to draw too much attention to it. He has Paul getting into enough trouble as it is. But the riot in the theatre in Ephesus, which Acts describes in chapter 19, may have been part of it. In that passage, things are quietened down by the city officials. But people had woken up to the fact that if the message Paul was announcing was to catch on, their businesses would suffer; so would their civic pride in the great temple of Diana. And the opposition may well have continued in new and nastier ways, leaving Paul feeling, as he says here, that he's received the sentence of death.

In fact, his description sounds much like what we would call a nervous breakdown. The load had become too heavy; all his natural human resources of energy and strength were worn down to nothing. It's bad enough to hear a magistrate declare that you are sentenced to death; it's far worse when a voice deep inside yourself tells you that you might as well give up and die. That is the point Paul had reached, the point where the night had become totally dark and all hope of dawn had disappeared.

Does that mean he'd been relying on his own resources up to that point? That sounds strange for someone who could write, in the previous letter, about his work being done not by his own efforts, but by God's grace (1 Corinthians 15.10). But maybe, beneath this conscious sense of God's help and grace, there was still more that Paul had to learn about the meaning of the **resurrection** – the very thing that he had made the climax of the earlier letter (chapter 15)! Here he says it

7

plainly: the fact that he came to the point where he despaired of life itself was somehow intended – intended by God, he must mean – to make him rely on 'the God who raises the dead'. This old Jewish belief in the life-giving God, the God whose power created the world and will recreate it, came home freshly to Paul as he found himself stripped of all other resources.

Paul begins his letter by telling them this much, not simply in order to gain sympathy, though no doubt that is part of it, but for two other reasons as well, one which he mentions and one which he doesn't. The one he mentions is that he wants them to be bound to him all the more tightly in a fellowship of prayer. When two people or communities pray seriously for one another, a bond is set up between them which transforms their relationship when they meet again. In addition, Paul sees in verse 11 that something else happens, which is what he is really interested in: when lots of people are praying for something, and God then grants it, there is all the more thanksgiving.

For Paul, when human beings give thanks to God, something at the heart of the universe comes back into proper shape. Humans thanking the creator for his goodness are a symptom of the way the world was meant to be, a sign that one day it really will be like that. And such signs are themselves powerful in helping forward the work of the **gospel** through which the great day will come. This theme of thanksgiving, to which Paul returns two or three more times in this letter, is one of several things that 2 Corinthians has in common with Colossians, which was perhaps written while Paul was in prison in Ephesus, shortly before his release. Then, some time after his release, he began to make his way round through Macedonia, intending to come south through Greece to Corinth. That's when he's writing this letter.

The thing he doesn't mention explicitly, but which would be an important factor in his mind and that of his readers, is that illness and suffering in the ancient world was regularly regarded as a sign of divine displeasure. Whatever it was that Paul had gone through, it would have been easy for his enemies, or those who were jealous of him, to think to themselves that it probably served him right, that God was most likely punishing him for something or other. Not so, says Paul. These things come not because God is angry but because he wants you to trust him the more fully. Many of the greatest saints and mystics (insofar as we have any idea what 'greatness' means in such cases) have spoken of a sense of darkness in which they discern the call of God to trust him beyond what they can see or imagine. This is something the ancient world had not thought of. Paul was breaking new ground. He wanted the Corinthians to understand that this, too, was part of the earth-shattering implication of the gospel.

He also yearned that they would abandon any lingering suspicions about his motives in preaching to them in the first place and in writing to them subsequently. We shall see later that some in Corinth have attacked him bitterly, sneering at him and implying all sorts of things about his character and secret aims. At this point he simply lays down a first statement of how things have been. His conscience is clear; he isn't trying to hide anything; he wants there to be complete understanding between them. After all, on the day when the Lord Jesus is revealed, the day Paul spoke of so often in the first letter, the churches in Greece will be his pride and joy, the sign that he has been faithful to his Lord and has discharged his commission. And he longs that they will see him that way too: their loyalty to him as their founding **apostle** will be the sign, on that day, that they really were and are following the Lord of whom he had spoken.

We have learned a lot about suffering, especially mental suffering, in the last century or so. Psychologists and psychiatrists, though sometimes producing some peculiar theories,

9

have given us real insight and brought much help and understanding to people in need. But this passage, though brief, goes as deep in its description of the problem and its solution as any modern theory. At the centre of everything are the issues of life and death. To face death, a sentence of death coming from one's own being, is as low as one can get. To trust in the God who raises the dead, with that **faith** anchored in the resurrection of Jesus himself, is the best therapy anyone could discover, in the first century or the twenty-first.

2 CORINTHIANS 1.15–22

Paul's Plans and God's 'Yes'

[15]I was quite sure of this. That's why I wanted to come to you again, so that you could have a double blessing. [16]I intended to go on to Macedonia by way of you, and to come back to you from Macedonia and have you send me on to Judaea.

[17]Was I just fooling around when I was making plans like this? Was I concocting schemes in a merely human way, prepared to say 'Yes, yes', and 'No, no', at the same moment? [18]God can bear me faithful witness that our word to you was not a mixture of Yes and No. [19]The son of God, Jesus the Messiah, who was proclaimed among you by Silvanus, Timothy and myself, wasn't a Yes-and-No person; in him it's always Yes! [20]All God's promises, you see, find their Yes in him; and that's why we say the Yes, the Amen through him when we pray to God and give him glory. [21]It's God who strengthens us with you into the Messiah, the anointed one; and he has anointed us, too. [22]God has stamped his seal on us, by giving us the spirit in our hearts as a first payment of what is to come.

One of my students once arrived very late for a tutorial. I was working on an extremely tight schedule, and I wasn't amused at having the day disrupted. I thought the student needed to know how far out of line his behaviour was.

I had just finished my little moral lecture, and we were beginning the tutorial, when the telephone rang. It was a publisher, wondering why I had not sent the writing I should have finished the previous month. I heard myself making the same kind of excuses the student had made to me a moment earlier.

I put the phone down, and we looked at each other.

'I feel a bit better now,' he said, with the hint of a smile.

I was reminded of this when imagining how frustrated the Corinthian church must have felt at Paul's various changes of plan. He seemed to be switching to and fro and they didn't know why. Recently I found myself caught up in a small-scale version of the same thing: my plans to travel to a speaking engagement next month were almost finalized, but a new opportunity arrived for something else as well, and maybe I should change the arrangements and stay on for two more days . . . As I made the necessary calls I thought how much easier it would have been if Paul had had a telephone or even email.

The Corinthian church had clearly been upset to get messages saying – so it seemed – first one thing and then another. To get from Ephesus to Corinth by sea wasn't difficult (see the map, p. xi). It's about two hundred and fifty miles, more or less due west, with the boat no doubt stopping here and there on the way through the Greek islands. Traders made the journey all the time. Paul himself had done it not long before, as we shall see, making a quick but painful visit which still reverberated through his memory and that of the church.

He had originally thought that he would go that route again: straight across to Corinth, north by land to Macedonia (to his dear friends in Thessalonica and Philippi), and then back to Corinth again, before setting off for Judaea once more. But something had happened to make him change his mind; and now he was coming the long way, by the land route around the northern Aegean. Travelling by land was usually slower and more dangerous than by sea, and Paul must have had good reason for the change of plan. Maybe his terrible experiences in Ephesus had left him unwilling to face a sea voyage just at the moment. But there may have been another reason too. If he travelled by land, he could send messengers ahead to prepare the Corinthians for his visit. After the disaster last time, he didn't want to risk just showing up and finding them unprepared.

But, though he has good reasons for his change of plan, the Corinthians have got the impression that he is vacillating, unable to make his mind up, perhaps deliberately sending mixed signals about his intentions. He's like a person who says 'Yes, yes', out of one side of the mouth and 'No, no', out of the other. Not so, Paul declares: I have always had Yes as my answer to you. It may come out in different ways, but I have been completely consistent. He has lived, prayed, and planned on the basis of the **gospel** itself; and the gospel is all about God saying Yes to people through the gospel of his **son**, the **Messiah**.

There is a triple Yes involved in the gospel. First, there is the Yes to all the promises God made in the Bible. For over a thousand years Israel had lived on those promises, trusting that the God who had called Israel to be his people would lead them forward, and accomplish in the end what he had planned and purposed. Paul's whole life was built on the belief that in Jesus of Nazareth God had done exactly that: Jesus was the Messiah, the culmination and crown of Israel's long story, the answer to all Israel's hopes and prayers, the fulfilment of all the promises. God had finally said Yes, and had said it so loudly through Jesus' **resurrection** that it was now echoing all around the world.

The second Yes is the one that those who believe in Jesus say when they pray. The Hebrew or Aramaic word for 'Yes' is 'Amen'. 'Amen' is one of the few Hebrew words spoken around

12

the world today, though most people don't realize where it comes from. When someone says a prayer, and other people want to associate themselves with it, they say 'Amen' at the end: it means 'Yes!' or 'I agree!' or 'That's what I want to say, too!' But Paul goes further. When we pray to the one true God, and give him glory, he says, we say the 'Amen' *through* Jesus the Messiah. When a prayer today ends with the words 'through Jesus **Christ** our Lord, Amen', the church is continuing a tradition which was well established when Paul was writing this letter, a mere twenty-five years or so after Jesus' death and resurrection, and which has continued in an unbroken line ever since. And the point of it is based on the first Yes. If the one true God has fulfilled his promises through the Messiah, Jesus, then when his people pray to him the appropriate way to ask is 'through Jesus the Messiah'.

The third Yes, therefore, is the one that reaches out from God to individual people today. What we need, if we are followers of the Messiah and learning what it means to belong to him, is to grow up 'into' him. The Messiah, as God's anointed king, represents his people, sums them up in himself, so that what is true of him becomes true of them. Christians need, therefore, to be strengthened 'into' the Messiah, and God's Yes to us today is what does that.

Paul even declares that, as Messiah means 'the anointed one', so God has 'anointed' the Messiah's people, too, by giving them his own **spirit** (verse 21). There are three ideas here, each of which is important for what comes later.

First, all God's people are 'anointed'. That is, they are themselves marked out by God, just as a king or a **priest** might have been. This is another way of saying what Paul says elsewhere when he sees Christians as the younger brothers and sisters of Jesus the Messiah.

Second, God has stamped us with his seal. Until comparatively modern times people who sent important letters would often seal them with molten wax, into which they would press a stamp or signet ring so that whoever got the letter would know who it had come from, and that it hadn't been tampered with on the way. God has 'sealed' his people with the spirit, and the stamp which the world will see on them is the mark of the Messiah himself, whose death and life they now share.

Third, the gift of the spirit is a first payment of what is to come. When people make large purchases, they often do so by putting down a lump sum in advance and thereby agreeing to pay off the rest in due time. When God anoints someone with the spirit, Paul declares, this is the first part of the gift which will be completed in the resurrection itself. If the Christian hope is founded on Jesus' own resurrection, that hope becomes a real possession within us through God's gift of the spirit.

Paul has moved from the Corinthians' puzzlement about his travel plans to the very centre of the gospel and the hope it brings. This is quite deliberate. He doesn't want the Corinthians to think of him, his travels and his forthcoming visit in purely human terms. He is anxious that they should learn to think of him, as they should learn to think of everything, in the light of God's great Yes in the gospel and the spirit.

2 CORINTHIANS 1.23—2.4

Painful Visit, Painful Letter

[23]For my own part, I call on God as witness, against my own life, that the reason I haven't yet come back to Corinth is because I wanted to spare you. [24]This isn't because I am making myself the lord and master over your faith; your faith is the reason you stand fast! Rather, it's because we are co-operating with you for your joy.

[2.1]You see, I settled it in my mind that I wouldn't make you another sad visit. [2]After all, if I make you sad, who is there to cheer *me* up except the one who is sad because of me? [3]And I wrote what I did so that I wouldn't come and find sadness where I should have found joy. I have this confidence about all of you, that my joy belongs to all of you. [4]No: I wrote to you in floods of tears, out of great trouble and anguish in my heart, not so that I could make you sad but so that you would know just how much overflowing love I have towards you.

I was trying to hang a picture and just couldn't get it right. I didn't calculate the height accurately enough, and when I stood back I realized it had to be about an inch higher up. Then when I tried to move the picture-hook some of the plaster in the wall came away; and when I put the hook where it should be, and began to hammer in the hook once more, another whole piece of plaster came loose. I stood back again in frustration. I had been trying to put things right, and what I had done seemed instead to have put them completely wrong. I had to get some filler and mend the hole, and then wait a day or two until it had hardened, before, this time, calculating the exact spot and nailing the hook extremely carefully where it should go.

I am (as this story will make clear) an amateur when it comes to do-it-yourself home improvements, even hanging pictures. But Paul was an **apostle**, called and equipped by God . . . surely he wouldn't have made basic mistakes? Part of what he's saying in this passage is that sometimes when bad things happen it doesn't mean that anybody's made a mistake: I couldn't have known that bit of the wall had some loose plaster; Paul couldn't have imagined that the Corinthians were in the wrong frame of mind for the kind of visit he planned; many things happen that are not what we would have expected or wanted, and we have to do the best we can with things as they are.

What Paul is beginning to do in this passage is, as it were, to put some new filling into an ugly crack in the wall, in the hope that it will set firm and enable him to make a fresh start with the work of building up the church. Last time he came, and last time he wrote, it all seemed to go horribly wrong.

Precisely what had happened is once more a matter of informed guesswork. Paul had made a brief visit to Corinth, coming, we assume, by the short sea route rather than the long way over land. He had hoped to be able to sort out some of the problems he had written about in the first letter. But instead of the church welcoming him with delight, and co-operating in putting things straight, there was opposition. Many people resented his intrusion. Some of the teachers who had arrived since he had left mocked his speaking style, his insignificant appearance. The tension between the cultural standards Corinth prided itself on and the strange new world of the Christian **gospel** were pulling at either end of the relationship between Paul and the church, and they came unstuck. We don't know the details, but we do know that it was very painful for everyone.

Paul returned to Ephesus, we assume, in deep distress, and wrote another letter, with tears rolling down his cheeks as he did so. Some people think that this 'painful' letter is actually now part of what we call '2 Corinthians', perhaps all or part of what we call chapters 10 to 13. That seems unlikely to me. It's more likely the letter wasn't preserved. We don't know what exactly he said, but we know what he hoped for. He hoped the letter would do the trick and make them see that he had acted out of deep love, not wanting to treat them as his private property, or to patronize them, or to upset them for the sake of it. And we know what it achieved: nothing, or rather worse than nothing. That, presumably, is why it wasn't preserved. Paul, by trying to make things better, had made them worse. He had now knocked a lump of plaster out of the wall, and was going to have to do some serious repair work.

Meanwhile, the storm that had been brewing in Ephesus,

16

whatever it was, had begun to break over his head. This was all he needed: trouble on the spot, and rebellion across the sea. No wonder he found himself sinking into the blackest depths of despair. And then, when he did get a message to them again, it was first to say that he was coming soon, then that he wasn't. And they just thought he was making it even worse.

No, he says: it was to spare you that I decided not to come after all (verse 23). Paul, emerging from the dark tunnel of depression, clinging for dear life to the God who raises the dead, still knows that this God has given him authority, with the spiritual power to back it up, to build up the church; and that means, if necessary, confronting evil wherever it occurs. He comes back to this theme at the end of the letter, in chapter 13, but we are aware of it at several points on the way as well. What he says, and the way he says it, speaks volumes about the nature of power within the Christian community.

We who live in a world that has known both violent revolutions and cruel tyrannies have grown cynical about all power. We always assume that anyone who says 'I'm doing this for your own good' is in fact manipulating us, twisting our arms to make us do something for their good rather than ours. Some have even suggested that Paul was up to the same trick. But Paul's whole point, throughout this letter, is that this is not the kind of power he has, or wants to have. He has no intention of playing the high-and-mighty lord and master over their **faith**; the faith they have is the faith by which they stand fast as genuine Christians, and it isn't his business to interfere with that, to come between them and the Lord himself. Rather, as a servant of the Lord on their behalf, he has a responsibility to work together with them, to increase their love and loyalty, and thereby also their joy.

This is because the kind of power that matters in Christian circles is the power of love. Paul's understanding of his relationship with the Corinthians is a rich interweaving of love and sorrow – which inevitably reminds us of the love and sorrow which met in Jesus himself at his death. He has acted, he says, not as part of a power-trip but because he loves them, and wants to see the sorrow turn to joy. He knows and believes that this can and will now happen. But, as Paul knows, and every experienced pastor knows, there is often a long, anxious moment when, to return to the picture hanging on the wall, we stand back and wonder whether this time it's going to be all right.

2 CORINTHIANS 2.5–11

Time to Forgive

5But if anyone has caused sadness, it isn't me that they have saddened, but, in a measure (I don't want to emphasize this too much), all of you. 6The punishment that the majority has imposed is quite enough; 7what's needed now is rather that you should forgive and console him, in case someone like that might be swallowed up by such abundant sorrow. 8Let me urge you, then, to reaffirm your love for him.

9The reason I wrote to you, you see, was in order to know whether you would pass the test and be obedient in everything. 10If you forgive anyone anything, so do I; and whatever I have forgiven – if indeed I have forgiven anyone anything! – it's all happened under the eyes of the Messiah, and for your own sake. 11The point is that we shouldn't be outsmarted by the satan. We know what he's up to!

'What can I do for you, then?' The doctor smiled over his spectacles.

'It's my memory,' said the patient. 'I just can't remember things like I used to.'

'How long has this problem been going on?' asked the doctor.

The patient looked puzzled.

'What problem?' he replied.

One of countless well-worn jokes about a problem we all discover as we get older. But remembering and forgetting isn't just a matter of increasing years (and perhaps the increasing amount of information we stuff into our heads these days). It can be a matter of the will. If you really want to remember something, you can often make the effort and do so. That doesn't surprise us too much. But, more surprisingly, you can *intend* to forget something, and actually succeed. You might think that the more you thought about your intention to forget it, the more you would in fact remember it. No doubt that sometimes happens, too. But it is one of the core disciplines of the Christian life that, with certain things, we should intend to forget them, and succeed.

The things in question are of course the bad things that other people have done which have affected us in some way. If you cling on to them, if you turn them over and over in your mind, they will go on having a bad effect on you. You are, in fact, going on giving the other people power to change and harm your life. But if you learn to let them go, you are free. Forgiveness is a two-way street: by releasing the other person from guilt, you release yourself from being crippled by their actions.

As a throwaway line in the middle of verse 10, Paul demonstrates that he has done this. 'Whatever I've forgiven', he begins, and then racks his brain to see if he has in fact forgiven anyone anything. He assumes he must have done, but he can't for the life of him think who or what it is. 'If indeed I have forgiven anyone anything!' he adds. This isn't absent-mindedness. It is part of a rigorous spiritual discipline. When Paul forgives, he also forgets.

That may seem a hard and high standard to aim for, but it shows the calibre of person we are dealing with when we're reading Paul. It also shows the astonishing standard he is setting for the community that follows Jesus, then and now. The question at issue here is the double one: how should the Corinthian church now behave towards a member who has been put under severe discipline for seriously bad behaviour? And how should the church itself respond to Paul's command that they exercise that discipline in the first place?

The person in question may perhaps be the same person Paul denounced in 1 Corinthians 5.1–5, the man who had been living with his father's wife. He had then instructed that the man should be dismissed from the Christian fellowship, put out into the dark world beyond the reach of grace – a strange and terrible notion, foreign to much of today's Christianity, where moral standards have declined to the point where all kinds of deviant behaviour are tolerated and even celebrated. We are left as usual to fill in the gaps between 1 Corinthians and 2 Corinthians; perhaps the church had initially refused to discipline the man, standing up to Paul when he made his short and painful visit, and then finally responding after the 'sorrowful letter' he referred to in the previous verses. We do not know. What we do know is that, in response to one of Paul's appeals, the church did indeed put someone under extremely severe discipline, so severe that Paul now sees he needs to take them on to the next stage, that of reconciliation and forgiveness.

What they must realize is the extent to which the community's life is bound up together, so that what happens to one member affects everybody. If one is sorrowful, a blight is cast over them all. However, if one is allowed licence to go on sinning without restraint, the whole community is pulled down into the mud. Holding these two together requires a Christian community to think in terms of an ongoing story rather than a snapshot moment: it may be necessary *first* to confront and discipline a persistent sinner, and *then* to deal with the sorrow that results. Too often the church, at least in the mainstream of modern Western Christianity, has been so anxious about ever causing sorrow to anyone that it has backed off from confrontation and discipline. Sometimes the opposite mistake is made, of course. But Paul's point is that the right sequence, and balance, needs to be maintained. And he himself is an example of how it's done.

Forgive – and forget. Of course, if the discipline has only gone skin deep, and the offender returns quickly to the same practices, something more may need to be done. The balance of wisdom and love will always need to be fine-tuned as the story develops. But none of this, in any case, is simply a matter of 'getting things right' in church life for the sake of order and tidiness. It has to do with a larger and darker issue. It is about the church's stand against the accuser, the **satan**. We know, Paul says, the cunning plans he is working out. We mustn't let ourselves be outwitted by him.

Behind every issue of behaviour and discipline within the church there stands the larger issue, of what the living God is doing in this community, and in particular through this community in the world. If the community is simply concerned to have a placid life, and tones down the clear and definite notes of **gospel** belief and behaviour for the sake of that, its effectiveness, its witness and mission to the world, will be greatly reduced. The satan will be delighted. Equally, if a community becomes so keen on discipline and order that it deals harshly with offenders and allows them no chance to repent, to make amends, and to be welcomed back as full members, the satan will be just as pleased. Somehow the church must steer the course between these two, with a touch on the tiller first this way and then that. If it doesn't, it will simply go round in circles. And worse.

Ultimately – this is a major theme of this letter – the church must remember that, whatever it does, it does under the gaze of the **Messiah** himself (verse 10). Paul's own life is lived in that gaze, as he says several times (see especially 4.6); and it is lived 'for your sake'. There comes a point when the church either has to trust Paul that he really means this, or to collapse into endless suspicions and recriminations. Such questions of trust remain at the heart of all the pastoral work, at whatever level, that today's church so badly needs.

2 CORINTHIANS 2.12–17

The Smell of Life, the Smell of Death

[12]However, when I came to Troas to announce the Messiah's gospel, and found an open door waiting for me in the Lord, [13]I couldn't get any quietness in my spirit because I didn't find my brother Titus there. So I left them and went off to Macedonia.

[14]But thanks be to God – the God who always leads us in his triumphal procession in the Messiah, and through us reveals everywhere the sweet smell of knowing him. [15]We are the Messiah's fragrance before God, you see, to those who are being saved and to those who are being lost. [16]To the latter, it's a smell which comes from death and leads to death; but to the former it's the smell of life which leads to life.

Who can rise to this challenge? [17]We aren't mere pedlars of God's word, as so many people are. We speak with sincerity; we speak from God; we speak in God's presence; we speak in the Messiah.

'What does that remind you of?'

The smell came strongly to me, a dark, heavy but essentially friendly aroma.

I thought for a while. Pictures flashed to and fro in my memory.

I sniffed again. Then, as though from far away, I saw myself standing in a room with the sunlight flooding in through a French window. A grand piano. A glass-fronted bookcase. A fire in the grate. And somewhere in the room – perhaps on the tables at the side, covered with cut flowers and photographs – someone had been using a particular furniture polish. The smell had taken me right back not only to the visual memory, but to the boyhood emotions of security and enjoyment, memories of holidays and games and good food, of grandparents, uncles and aunts. Smells can penetrate recesses of memory and imagination that the other senses can't get near. And that's so even for us humans. I sometimes wonder what it's like being a dog.

The sense of smell was highly valued in the ancient world. The very mention of 'sweet-smelling knowledge' in this passage could have awakened many different associations in the minds of an ancient reader. Paul may well have more than one of these in mind.

They might have thought of **sacrifice** in a temple, perhaps in the **Temple** in Jerusalem. People believed that the divinity would smell the sweet smell of the sacrifice and be pleased with it, as Genesis 8.21 says about God's reaction to the sacrifice of Noah. Paul uses this idea elsewhere, as in Philippians 4.18, where he likens the gift he'd received from Philippi to a sweet-smelling sacrifice that God enjoys.

Or they might simply have thought of incense, which was regularly used to indicate the presence of the divinity, in both pagan and Jewish worship. Paul's meaning would then be that, as he announces the **gospel**, the effect is like the smell of a sacrifice, or of incense, which rises up in worship to God and lets everybody around know that God is present.

But neither of these quite explains the sharp distinction he makes between the effect of the smell on those who are being saved and its effect on those who are being lost. To explain that, we need to put together the idea of the sweet smell with the idea at the beginning of verse 14: that God is 'leading us in his triumphal procession'.

Most people in Paul's world would know about triumphal processions. When a king, a general, or some other great leader had won a notable military victory, the whole city would turn out to welcome him and his troops as they came home in jubilation. They would bring with them the prisoners they had taken; they would display the booty they had plundered; and they would do everything to make it clear to their own people that they had indeed been victorious. All kinds of ceremonies and rituals were devised to make the point, and among them was the practice of the burning of incense. This celebrated the arrival of the triumphant general; it spoke to people in the crowds, and in neighbouring streets, of what was happening, whether they could see it or not. It reminded the victors of their victory, and the rewards that awaited them; and it reminded the conquered prisoners of their defeat, and the fate that lay in store for them. Prisoners were usually killed, perhaps by being forced to fight wild animals in the amphitheatre. Alternatively, they might be sold into slavery.

Paul is often happy to mix ideas together. It's quite likely that he is thinking primarily of one of these images, probably the military triumph which he begins with in verse 14, while allowing other ideas to come in as well. His point is that, as God's triumphal procession makes its way through the world following the victory of Jesus the **Messiah** over death and sin, people like himself, who are in the procession, are wafting the smell of victory, the smell of triumph, to people all round. To those who are being grasped by the love and power of the gospel and who are responding to it, the smell is sweet: it means victory, joy, hope and peace even in the middle of present troubles. To those who are setting their faces against the gospel and all that it means, the same smell reminds them that the victory God won in the Messiah means victory over all the forces that oppose his healing rule of justice and peace;

in other words, that those who oppose are signing their own death warrant.

We shouldn't be surprised that this makes him ask, as anyone might: Who can rise to this challenge? Who can possibly live up to it? The obvious answer, of course, is: Nobody can – unless God comes to their help. That, indeed, is what Paul himself says in the next passage. But here he is content simply to conclude by saying, in effect: Well, with a calling like this, with a commission from God, in the presence of God, as a member of the Messiah's people, we have no choice but to obey. And, as we obey, we do so with sincerity (a point Paul has already stressed in 1.12). Whoever has been stirring up suspicion against Paul, their accusations are unfounded. He contrasts himself in verse 17 with the kind of people who offer something they call God's **word** for sale, like traders on a street corner, charging what they can get and not worrying too much about the quality of what they give. Paul is not that kind of person.

The opening lines of the passage describe Paul's anxious journey, north from Ephesus to Troas (ancient Troy, near the coast), then across to Macedonia. He was anxious because he had sent Titus ahead of him to Corinth, to find out the current mood, and tell him what sort of reception he might expect. He had thought that Titus would be coming back and would meet him at Troas, but he wasn't there. We have to wait until chapter 7 verse 5 to pick up the thread of this travel story again, with Titus finally meeting Paul and bringing good news. But at this point in the letter Paul pauses, in order to write one of his greatest extended discussions, this time on what precisely it means to be an **apostle**, a servant or minister of God's new **covenant**. Only if the Corinthians understand this will they be in a position to understand all the other things he wants to say to them.

2 CORINTHIANS 3.1–6

The Letter and the Spirit

[1]So: we're starting to 'recommend ourselves' again, are we? Or perhaps we need – as some do – official references to give to you? Or perhaps even to get from you? [2]*You* are our official reference! It's written on our hearts! Everybody can know it and read it! [3]It's quite plain that you are a letter from the Messiah, with us as the messengers – a letter not written with ink but with the spirit of the living God, not on tablets of stone but on the tablets of beating hearts.

[4]That's the kind of confidence we have towards God, through the Messiah. [5]It isn't as though we are qualified in ourselves to reckon that we have anything to offer on our own account. Our qualification comes from God: [6]God has qualified us to be stewards of a new covenant, not of the letter but of the spirit. The letter kills, you see, but the spirit gives life.

I had to write a letter of recommendation last week. One of my former students is job-hunting, and the people who run the college he has applied to don't know him, or not very well; so it is up to me to write to them, in a formal way, to set out the qualifications of the man concerned, as well as the less easily definable things that we loosely call 'character'. Even though in the modern world people can find out a good deal about one another by various other means, we still rely quite a lot, in making appointments, on official letters.

How much more was this necessary in the ancient world, before electronic communications, when people who travelled as part of their work (not many people, except the very rich, travelled for pleasure in those days) often had to carry official letters to say who they were, what their business was, and so on. In the early church itself, as we know from the early Christian document called the *Didache* or 'Teaching of the Twelve **Apostles**', the practice of writing letters of recommendation was a way of making sure that people who showed up out of the blue, claiming to be servants of Jesus the **Messiah**, were actually genuine.

Now on one occasion, earlier in my teaching career, I had some dealings with a man who had been in business, had become involved in some illegal practices, and had served time in prison as a result. When he came out, he was eager to get back into employment, but didn't want to tell potential employers about the unfortunate gap in the middle of his life history; so he gave them the names and addresses of people who would write references for him – but they were all fictitious. The letters came to him personally, and he was intending to write 'letters of recommendation' on his own behalf, pretending that they came from qualified persons who would vouch for some tale about where he had been in recent years.

As soon as this fraud was discovered, he disappeared, and I haven't heard from him since. But this kind of deceit, writing on your own behalf, seems to have been what the Corinthians were accusing Paul of. Perhaps after reading passages like the first four chapters of 1 Corinthians, and chapter 9 as well, they might have sneered that he seemed to be writing references for himself, telling everybody what a good fellow he was. And now Paul is anxious that from what he's just said, in defending himself against the slanders that some have been uttering, he will be opening himself to the charge of writing another self-recommendation. This charge clearly hurt, because he comes back to it on several subsequent occasions (4.2; 5.12; 6.4; 10.12, 18; 12.11). In fact, it seems as though this question is one of the most basic ones that the letter is written to answer.

Nor is it simply that some people have accused him of writing self-congratulatory, self-recommending letters. Some people – unless this is Paul being even more sarcastic than we might imagine – are actually suggesting that if Paul wants to come back to Corinth, after all that's happened between them,

27

he should get someone, perhaps the church in Ephesus, to write an official letter to give him accreditation! Or maybe that if he wants to work as an apostle anywhere else they themselves, the church in Corinth, should graciously give him such a letter!

Paul responds in the only way he can. But, in responding, he sets off on a journey of explanation in which he goes down to the depths of what being an apostle is all about. As so often in the history of the church, it's only when something really outrageous is said that a true theologian is stirred to write something which explains what up until then, one might have thought, had been assumed, but obviously hadn't been. And in this case the central thing is the new **covenant**.

The new covenant! Paul, as so often, is deeply rooted in the Old Testament; and the passage where the new covenant is promised is Jeremiah 31. Faced with imminent **exile**, the punishment for Israel's persistent and unrepentant covenant-breaking, the prophet promises that one day YHWH will restore the fortunes of Israel by bringing about a new covenant, a new agreement between himself and Israel, a new marriage of God and God's people. The old covenant was the one made by God through Moses, but it didn't have the power to make the people everything that God longed for them to be. The new covenant will therefore have a negative and positive task: negatively, it must deal with the sins which the people had committed; positively, it must establish the relationship between God and Israel on an entirely new footing. Something must be done to create a new sort of people, a people who will be alive with God's own **life**. Jeremiah spoke of this in terms of God putting his **law** into people's hearts, and that is very close to what Paul envisages here. But the central thing he has to say, the central contrast between the old covenant and the new one, is that now God will give his own **spirit** to his people.

This is the heart of Paul's response to the charge. This is

why he can say, so dramatically, in verse 2, that *you* – you Corinthians, you muddled, beloved, infuriating, joyful Corinthians – you are my letter of recommendation. If anybody wants to find out what sort of a person Paul is, what sort of a Christian worker he is, then they should look at the church in Corinth and draw their conclusions. That is quite a frightening thought, considering the trouble Paul was having with them; but it puts them nicely on the spot. Has he not told them to copy his own lifestyle (1 Corinthians 10.31)? Well then, people should be able to find out about Paul by looking at the Corinthians.

If they are a 'letter', it's a letter from the Messiah himself, written by the spirit: a letter to the whole world, declaring 'the man who founded this community is a genuine apostle of Jesus the Messiah'. Or is that what it will say? Will it say, perhaps, 'the man who founded this community was a muddled, self-seeking petty dictator'? What do they want it to say? What *ought* they to want it to say?

Paul, with extraordinary boldness, is quietly confident that the letter will in fact tell the truth; because he knows that the living God has performed a powerful work among people in Corinth, writing this 'letter' not on tablets of stone – this is where he is starting to contrast the 'new covenant' with the covenant of Moses – but on tablets of living, beating hearts, 'hearts of flesh' as a more literal translation would have it. The new marriage-covenant God has made with his people – and his people are now a worldwide family, not of Jews only but of all who believe – is inscribed in the innermost beings of those who believe. It isn't that they've had a new religious experience which might last, say, a week or even a year. It is that the living God has written something in their hearts, so that they can never be the same people again.

This, then, is Paul's 'qualification', answering the question of 2.16. Paul is not 'qualified' in any human sense; nobody could be. His 'qualification' comes from God, and God alone. And the only 'letter of recommendation' he needs, the only one he could ever have, is written not with paper and ink, not even with a chisel in a stone tablet like the law of Moses, but in the living beings, the persons, the prayers, the decisions, the love, of this community in Corinth, where to date he had done his most thorough work. 'The letter kills, but the spirit gives life'; in other words, as he says in Romans 8, God has now done 'what the law could not do'. God has given new life where the law of Moses had not been able to. The **resurrection** of Jesus unleashed life into the world; Paul and the other apostles are simply the stewards, the household servants, of this new life as it bubbles up to refresh the whole world. That is Paul's quali-fication; and that is the single vital qualification for ministers of the **gospel** from that day to this.

2 CORINTHIANS 3.7–11

Death and Glory

[7]But just think about it: when death was being distributed, carved in letters of stone, it was a glorious thing, so glorious in fact that the children of Israel couldn't look at Moses's face because of the glory of his face – a glory that didn't last. [8]But in that case, when the spirit is being distributed, won't that be glorious too? [9]If distributing condemnation is glorious, you see, how much more glorious is it to distribute vindication! [10]In fact, what used to be glorious has come in this respect to have no glory at all, because of the new glory which goes so far beyond it. [11]For if the thing which was to be abolished came with glory, how much more glory will there be for the thing that lasts.

The two teenagers were slumped in armchairs. Both of them had their headphones plugged into personal stereos, and had the faraway look of people being carried along by hidden sounds. One of them nodded her head gently in time with the beat. The other was clicking his fingers.

Neither gave any attention to what was happening at the other end of the room. There, at the piano, sat a guest of the family. The family hadn't realized she was a famous pianist; she was a friend of a friend, who had needed a place to stay for a couple of nights. She was now practising for a concert. The gentle, powerful music flowed around the room, out into the hallway, and up the stairs, filling the house with beauty as surely as if all the spring flowers in the garden had suddenly released their scent.

The lady of the house came downstairs, entranced. She stopped in the doorway and looked at her two children with a mixture of amusement and horror. Then she beckoned them to come out of the room.

'Don't you realize what you're missing?' she whispered.

The older one, lip-reading her mother because the stereo was still filling her head with heavy rock, frowned.

'What d'you mean?' she said.

'What I mean', said her mother, 'is that there is great music in this house, and you're missing it!'

The younger one took off his headphones and listened for a minute.

'That's not real music,' he said. 'That's just tinkly little tunes.'

And he replaced the headphones.

The mother tried again.

'Listen,' she said. 'What you've got in your heads will last for five minutes. Next week it'll be a different song and you'll forget this one. What she's playing in there will last for ever. People have loved that music for centuries already, and they'll go on loving it for many more!'

'Let them,' replied the boy. 'It doesn't do anything for me.'

I know the illustration is imperfect. The contrast Paul is

making is deeper and more important than the contrast between rock music, which lasts for a few weeks, and the glorious music of the great composers. The musical contrast can be associated with a cultural snobbery which Paul would have hated. But the picture of the frustrated mother, trying to persuade her couldn't-care-less children that listening to great music is actually far more glorious than listening to pop, is something like the picture of Paul, trying to get the message across to the Corinthians that the distribution of the **spirit** is a far more glorious thing than the distribution of death; that the 'new **covenant**' God has made in Jesus the **Messiah** is a far more glorious thing than the 'old covenant' he made with Israel through Moses.

The contrast seems obvious to us – no doubt because Paul has put it in such a way that it's hard to disagree – but it wasn't to them. What isn't obvious to us is why Paul needed to stress the point in this way. Were there, perhaps, people in Corinth who had been teaching the young church that they should observe the **law** of Moses? There is no reason – other than this passage itself – to think so. (In 11.22 he speaks of some opponents who are clearly Jews, but this isn't a reason to suppose that they are teaching the kind of law-observance that the rival teachers in Galatia had been doing.)

I think it's more likely that Paul is simply wanting to get through to the Corinthians just what a glorious thing the new covenant is; and to do this he is telling, as he so often did, the story of the old covenant. Chapter 3 is, in fact, the first part of a long argument, which builds up step by step through to the great climax in 6.3–10, explaining to the Corinthians that the life and work of a genuine **apostle** of Jesus the Messiah *really is a glorious thing, even though it doesn't look like it to them.* The Corinthians have allowed themselves to imagine that an apostle – a leader of this new movement that they'd joined – ought to conform to the standards of showy leadership, flowery and entertaining speaking, personal charm and flattery, that they were used to in their culture. What Paul ultimately wants to say to them is that all these things are like cheap pop music compared with the lifestyle which embodies the **gospel** of Jesus. At the moment they are (he implies) like sulky teenagers who don't want to listen to real music, who can't believe that it contains passion and glory, beauty and love beyond anything they've imagined. And the way he does this is to tell one part of the biblical story of Moses, and to contrast it with the story of the gospel and the spirit.

The part of the Moses-story he chooses is found in Exodus 34. Moses had been up on the mountain for a long time, receiving instructions from God about the building of the tabernacle, the place where God would come and live with his people. The people, however, persuaded Aaron to make a golden calf, an idol. The first word that Moses and his law had to utter to God's people was the word of condemnation, the announcement of death. Moses suddenly found himself in the position of counsel for the defence, pleading with God to spare his guilty people. This deep and heartfelt prayer called forth from God a fresh revelation of himself: Moses glimpsed God's glory, and heard the message that, though wickedness must be dealt with, God was indeed a God of overflowing mercy. And when Moses returned once more from the mountain-top, his face was shining, and the Israelites were afraid of him. So he covered his face with a veil, except for when he went in to the tabernacle where God made himself present, to speak with God face to face.

Paul's point, then, is that even this glorious revelation of God is as nothing compared with the glory which is revealed in the gospel, the **message** about Jesus, through which God's spirit is powerfully at work to bring **life** and vindication in place of death and condemnation. But, like the mother in the story, he has to make the point because of course it's not obvious to people whose minds and hearts are stuck in a different culture, a different set of assumptions. Paul's face does not literally shine as he speaks; the Corinthians might have sat up and taken more notice if it had. But Paul wants them to realize that when God is at work in them by his spirit there is a glory at work that puts even Moses in the shade.

Part of his whole argument, in fact, is that Christians have to get used to setting their course by what cannot be seen rather than what can (see 4.18); by what is going to last for ever, rather than by what lasts merely for a while; not by lifestyles and cultures which will end in death, but by what brings life the other side of death. Much of this letter is taken up with these themes, and Paul has here focused them sharply on the contrast between the admittedly glorious work of Moses and the apparently un-glorious work he had to do as an apostle. He is challenging them to look for the real glory even though at the moment they can't see it; to listen for the hidden power of the gospel music, even though at the moment their heads are filled with the transient power of what their culture gives them. It is a challenge the church needs to hear again and again.

2 CORINTHIANS 3.12–18

The Veil and the Glory

[12]So, because that's the kind of hope we have, we speak with great freedom. [13]We aren't like Moses: he put a veil over his face, to stop the children of Israel from gazing at the end of what was being abolished. [14]The difference is that their minds were hardened. You see, the same veil lies over the reading of the old covenant right up to this very day. It isn't taken away, because it's in the Messiah that it is abolished.

[15]Yes, even to this day, whenever Moses is read, the veil lies upon their hearts; [16]but 'whenever he turns back to the Lord,

the veil is removed'. [17]Now 'the Lord' here means the spirit; and where the spirit of the Lord is, there is freedom. [18]And all of us, without any veil on our faces, gaze at the glory of the Lord as in a mirror, and so are being changed into the same image, from glory to glory, just as you'd expect from the Lord, the spirit.

The story is told of a time when there was to be a total eclipse of the sun. The newspapers and the radio and television stations repeatedly put out warnings, reminding people that they should not attempt to look directly at the sun. Even ordinary sunglasses would not protect you if you tried to do that. You should always look through thick, darkened glass. Shops that sold the right protective glass did a brisk trade. The warnings kept coming. Finally a lady wrote to one of the national newspapers about it. If this eclipse was so dangerous, she said, why were we having one in the first place?

No doubt politicians and those who organize mass entertainments would love to be able to lay on something so spectacular as an eclipse. Fortunately, the really astonishing things in our world remain firmly outside our control. But the idea of protective screens that stop you being hurt by looking at something too bright, too glorious, is central here.

Moses, as we saw in the previous passage, had to put a veil over his face, to stop the children of Israel gazing at the shining glory which was coming from it as a result of his having been with God and even glimpsed God, albeit from behind. (If you go into an art gallery and look at pictures of Moses painted a few hundred years ago, you may see that he has little horns on his head. That's because the Latin word for 'veiled' is very like the Latin word for 'horned', and people who read the Bible in Latin became confused and thought it was saying that Moses had horns on his head.) The Israelites had to be prevented from looking at the glory. The point Paul is making is that his ministry, his work as an **apostle**, isn't like that. When he is at work, everyone must see the glory.

What he wants to stress in particular is that, because of the difference between his work and Moses's work, he must use great 'freedom' or 'boldness' when he speaks (verse 12). He mustn't hide the real **message**; he is under obligation to speak it out boldly and clearly, not masking it with clever tricks of speech. The Corinthians, we may assume, had criticized him for his blunt, clear, no-nonsense teaching. They would have preferred something more oblique, more fashionable, something less dazzling and inescapable, something less demanding. No, Paul declares: because we have this hope (he hasn't mentioned 'hope' in so many words in the passage before this, but the whole point of what he's been saying is that the new **covenant** is the guarantee of **life**, life that will last for ever), we have to speak boldly and plainly. And the reason for this is because of the work of the **spirit**: where the spirit of the Lord is (verse 17), there is freedom!

But how he gets to that point is the really interesting bit. We can easily assume, as we read this passage, that he is simply drawing a contrast between Moses and himself. We might guess, in advance of reading what he actually says, that he might be going to say that Moses has a rather second-rate ministry, whereas he, Paul, has a better one. He might be going to say that Moses doesn't have the same sort of glory that he, Paul, has. But wait a minute: the whole point was that Moses *did* have the glory! That was the problem! Moses had gazed upon God, and now his face was shining as a result. The problem wasn't with Moses; the problem was with everybody else, the great majority of the Israelites. As Paul insists in Romans 7, the problem wasn't with Moses and the **law**. The problem was (so to speak) with the raw material the law had to work with, that is, with the hard hearts of the people (verse 14).

So Paul takes the biblical picture of Moses and his veil and develops it two stages further. First, he says that since the problem which caused Moses to wear a veil in the first place was the state of heart of the people, we can see that the veil still lies over the law itself, the 'old covenant', when it is read in the synagogue. In other words, the law really would reveal God's glory; it really would point forward, like a great story in search of an ending, to the coming of the **Messiah**. But for those whose hearts are not ready for it, it is 'veiled'.

Second, therefore, it is as though the veil lies, not just over the law when it's read, but over their actual hearts (verse 15). Paul is not, of course, thinking of 'Jewish people' as though he wasn't one himself. He is describing the person he once was, unable to see or even imagine that the crucified Jesus of Nazareth could be God's Messiah, the one in whom Israel's hope and destiny found its fulfilment, the one in whom God said 'Yes' to all the old promises (1.20). He looks with sorrow, as he does in Romans 9.1–5, at his fellow-Jews, and longs that the veil should be removed.

But how can it be removed? Paul is still thinking of Exodus 34. In the story of Moses and the veil, the time Moses takes off the veil is when he goes back in to the tabernacle, into the presence of the Lord. The veil was needed because the people's hearts were hard, but you don't need the veil when face to face with the Lord. So Paul takes Exodus 34.34 ('whenever he turns back to the Lord, the veil is removed'), and quotes it with a wider meaning: now, whenever *anyone* turns to the Lord – the word 'turn' here could mean 'convert' or 'repent' – the veil is removed. (We should note the implication: that, when someone turns to the Lord, they will be able to understand the true meaning of the Bible.)

Paul, remember, is explaining the nature of his own ministry: it is a ministry without a 'veil', without any cloak of secrecy or rhetorical trickery. It is a ministry of 'boldness', 'freedom of speech', *because both he and his hearers are people who have* 'turned to the Lord' and whose hearts are therefore no longer hard. You don't need the protective screening, he says. You don't any longer need to look at the glory through a thick dark glass. The veil is removed.

But how can Paul make this text in Exodus refer to the relationship he has with his hearers? Because, he says, 'the Lord' in this text can be seen as a reference to the spirit, the sovereign one who softens hearts and changes lives, who brings new life in the present and guarantees it for the future (1.21–22). And this leads Paul to the most astonishing claim of the whole chapter (verse 18). When he looks at a congregation, and when they look at him, and when they look at one another, everybody is looking at somebody else in whose heart and life the spirit, the Lord, has been at work, to heal, to soften, to change, to give life – in other words, to give glory. Paul isn't talking about the way we gaze, by **faith**, on the face of the Lord. He isn't referring to the way we look at God, or Jesus. He is talking – this, after all, is the point of the whole chapter – about the way we gaze at the life-giving spirit in the faces of our fellow-Christians.

Think of it like this (adapting the illustration Paul himself uses in verse 18). When the sun rises in the morning, depending on what time of year it is, it often strikes the windows of one of my neighbours before it strikes mine. And his window reflects it right into my house. I look at my neighbour's house and see the brightness of the sun. Yes, says Paul: we gaze at the glory of the Lord as in a mirror; but, instead of being dazzled and needing to use a veil, we find ourselves, each one of us, being changed like Moses from one degree of glory to another, because of the Lord, the spirit, at work within us.

Of course, our faces don't normally shine in the way that Moses's did (though there are quite a few stories of Christians down the years to whom that has happened). But Paul's whole point is that this glory is something you recognize by faith.

And it's something you certainly don't want to hide by clever speech. The task of an apostle – of any true minister of the Christian **gospel** – is to be an agent of this new, and renewing, covenant; and that will mean boldness, face-to-face clear speech. And glory.

2 CORINTHIANS 4.1–6

Light out of Darkness

[1]For this reason, since we have this work entrusted to us in accordance with the mercy we have received, we don't lose heart. [2]On the contrary, we have renounced the secret things that make people ashamed. We don't use tricks; we don't falsify God's word. Rather, we speak the truth openly, and recommend ourselves to everybody's conscience in the presence of God.

[3]However, if our gospel still remains 'veiled', it is veiled for people who are perishing. [4]What's happening there is that the God of this world has blinded the minds of unbelievers, so that they won't see the light of the gospel of the glory of the Messiah, who is God's image. [5]We don't proclaim ourselves, you see, but Jesus the Messiah as Lord, and ourselves as your servants because of Jesus; [6]because the God who said 'let light shine out of darkness' has shone in our hearts, to produce the light of the knowledge of the glory of God in the face of Jesus the Messiah.

I walked into the smart office, slightly early for my appointment. The porter at the front door handed me on to an assistant, who walked with me up two grand flights of stairs and through an imposing door. It was a long time since I had met the woman who was now at the head of the organization, and I wasn't even sure I would recognize her.

As we came through the door a well-dressed woman of about the right age got up and walked towards us with a smile and an outstretched hand. Well, I thought, my memory wasn't too bad; she wasn't exactly as I remembered, but not all that far off. We shook hands. How very good to see you again, I said. She looked at me with a slight surprise, and then walked back across the room to an inner door, tapped gently on it, and opened it. There, in the inner room, sat the woman I had come to see. She hadn't changed a bit. I had mistaken a personal assistant for the head of the organization.

Paul is very concerned that the Corinthians might have supposed he regarded himself as the head of the organization. He is simply a servant, a porter, a secretary, an assistant: he is merely someone who introduces people to the top man. He is one of the **Messiah**'s office staff. Verse 5 says it all: We don't proclaim ourselves, but Jesus, the Messiah, as Lord! We have to introduce people to him, not to keep them in the outer office as though we ourselves were the people they should get to know. In fact, if we even began to do that we would be disloyal to our commission. Our job is to make Jesus known, and then to keep out of the way, to make sure we don't get in the light.

Because light is what this is all about. Paul may here be hinting at the moment at which, as he was filled with angry enthusiasm to persecute the young church, he was knocked to the ground by a blinding light that flashed from **heaven**, in which he saw the risen Jesus in all his glory. His life was transformed by that meeting, not just by the experience itself but by what he realized it meant. If Jesus was risen from the dead, he really was the Messiah. If he was the Messiah, he was the one in whom all God's purposes had come true. He was, in fact, God's **son**, God's image, God's new light . . .

In fact, he was the agent of God's new creation. The light that blinded Paul on the road to Damascus, the light that suddenly shone in people's hearts when he went around the world announcing the **gospel** of Jesus, was like the light at the very beginning, at the creation of the world. 'Let there be light,' commanded the creator God, and there was light (Genesis 1.3): a light which, as John says (John 1.5), shines in the darkness, and the darkness has not been able to put it out. With Jesus, God's new world comes into being. The gospel isn't about a different god, someone other than the world's original creator, but about the same creator God bringing new **life** and light to his world, the world where death and darkness have made their home and usurped his role. Paul summarizes God's command in Genesis 1, in order to say: what happened to me that day, what happened to you when you believed, and what happens whenever anyone 'turns to the Lord' (3.16), is a moment of new creation (see 5.17).

That is how Paul has come to believe that Jesus, the Messiah, is the one who reflects the living God himself. Only the living God can shine the light of new creation; and when you look at Jesus, as Paul had, face to face, you realize that you are looking at God's own glory. That gives you knowledge, knowledge of the innermost secrets of the universe, and God's saving plan for it; and in that knowledge there is more than enough light to see the way through the dark world. All of that is contained in the remarkable statement in verse 6.

This helps us to understand Paul's extraordinary confidence in verses 1 and 2. If you really believe that God has revealed himself like this in and through Jesus, and has entrusted you with the task of announcing this **good news** in the world, then you won't need to use the tricks of rhetoric. You won't need to play fast and loose either with the Bible itself or with the gospel **message**. You will simply need to speak it out, openly and unafraid. It is not, after all, a message from a god that nobody has any idea of. It is a message from the creator God, the one in whose image all human beings were made, the one of whom every human being is at least dimly aware. Everybody has a conscience to which this message will make its appeal, like a message from an almost-forgotten relative, awakening memories and hopes.

But not everybody reacts like this, as Paul himself knew only too well. Yes, he says, because the 'veil' doesn't just apply to Jewish people as he himself had been; it applies to people of all sorts. Tragically, there are many who remain blinded, 'veiled', by 'the god of this world'. That is one of Paul's ways of referring to the dark power, the **satan**, who opposes God's light and truth. Of course, Paul knew that, as in his own case, so in many others, the gospel could and did pierce the veil. But this is his way of making sure he doesn't fall into the trap of saying, on the one hand, that people who become Christians do so because they happen to have chosen one religious option among many, or, on the other, that the gospel of Jesus has no contact with the minds of ordinary people. It isn't so much that the gospel comes to people as a strange, alien invasion, forcing them into a mould for which they were not made. The strange, alien invasion is the one perpetrated by 'the god of this world', who stops people from seeing the healing, life-giving light of the gospel.

This passage, then, is central to Paul's view of his own job description. The Messiah is the full, true reflection of the one creator God in whose image all humans were made. To announce him is not to do something strange or outlandish, but to reveal the truth and the light that all people, however dimly, ought to recognize. Let nobody suppose that Paul is that light, or that truth. He doesn't go around talking about himself. He talks about Jesus.

2 CORINTHIANS 4.7–12

Treasure in Earthenware Pots

[7]But we have this treasure in earthenware pots, so that the extraordinary quality of the power may belong to God, not to

us. [8]We are under all kinds of pressure, but we are not crushed completely; we are at a loss, but not at our wits' end; [9]we are persecuted, but not abandoned; we are cast down, but not destroyed. [10]We always carry the deadness of Jesus about in the body, so that the life of Jesus may be revealed in our body. [11]Although we are still alive, you see, we are always being given over to death because of Jesus, so that the life of Jesus may be revealed in our mortal humanity. [12]So this is how it is: death is at work in us – but life in you!

Sir Oliver Franks was one of the most distinguised men in Oxford during my time as an undergraduate. He had been a professor of philosophy at an early age; he had been head of an Oxford college, still very young; he had been chairman of a major bank. Now he was back as head of another college, through the turbulent times of the late 1960s. But in between he had been selected for an even more demanding post, which he held in the all-important years shortly after the Second World War, at the time when the cold war began and the North Atlantic Treaty Organization was set up. He was British Ambassador to the United States.

As Ambassador, he was in touch, often on a daily basis, with the President on one side of the Atlantic and the Prime Minister on the other. He was the confidant of some of the most powerful people in the world. He frequently needed to get urgent, important and top secret messages to and fro between Washington and London. It was far too risky to make telephone calls; the line was almost certainly bugged. There was a diplomatic bag which went to and fro each day, bringing confidential documents by air across the Atlantic. That was the method he used for most of his important and confidential messages. But when something was really confidential, utterly top secret, and desperately urgent, he wouldn't trust it to a bag which everybody knew was important. He would put it into an ordinary envelope and send it through the regular mail.

What Paul is saying is that there is no chance of anyone confusing the content of the envelope with the very ordinary, unremarkable envelope itself. The messenger is not important; what matters, vitally and urgently, is the **message**. God's double bluff, as it were, to deceive the powers of the world, is like the Ambassador's double bluff to deceive potential enemy agents. The Corinthians have been looking at the envelope – at Paul's own public figure, his speaking style, and at the fact that he is in and out of trouble, weakness, and now near to death – and they have concluded that there is nothing at all remarkable about him. He ought to look more important than that, surely, if he really is a messenger with a message from the living God!

No, says Paul: you're missing the point. Precisely because of the vital importance of the message, the messenger must be dispensable. It's like putting treasure into clay pots or earthenware jars; they are fragile, breakable, disposable, but the treasure is what matters. If it were otherwise, the jars might regard themselves as important. The envelope might think that it was the letter. And so Paul begins the description of what life is like for a genuine **apostle**, a description that will continue on and off throughout the rest of the letter. The catalogue of suffering starts here, but goes on in chapters 6, 7 and 11 in particular. And he tells us, here at the start, the point of it all: the apostle finds himself modelled on the **gospel** itself, living it out in his own person, his own body. And he has come to believe that this is not an accident. It is part of the deal, part of the commission.

The gospel, of course, is the message of Jesus' death and **resurrection**. Everything Paul writes is based on those central events. Nowhere else, though, has he woven them into the very texture of his thinking and writing to the extent that he has done in this most personal letter, which seems at times to be welling up like a fountain of tears from the depths of his heart. 'The deadness of Jesus – that's what we carry about in the body; and this is in order that Jesus' **life** may be revealed there too!' That's what Paul has had to go through in Asia (1.8–10), and he is determined to understand his own experience not as a denial of the gospel but as a strange confirmation of it. If you want to see resurrection at work here and now, in your own life, you have to be prepared to see crucifixion at work as well. And if the Corinthians want an apostle who is living by the gospel he proclaims – Paul isn't sure that they do want this, but they ought to! – then they must look for these signs. Don't look, in other words, for a showy, flashy rhetorical presentation which leaves the problems and sufferings of the world to someone else. Look for someone who is being given over to death for the sake of Jesus, so that Jesus' life may be revealed even in their mortal humanity.

Somehow, strangely, this sense of death and life working together isn't just something which an individual can experience and know in themselves. It is something which affects those with and for whom he or she is working. Death, says Paul, is at work in us – but life in you! In other words, as he says in Colossians 1.24, his own sufferings are somehow, in the strange economy of God, taken up as part of the messianic sufferings of Jesus himself, whose death and life are present in his own body, and made to be effective for the benefit of the churches he has founded. How this happens remains a mystery. That it happens Paul has no doubt. But he doesn't want the Corinthians to misinterpret it. If he is suffering, while they are flourishing, this doesn't mean they are superior mortals and he is inferior. It means that there is a strange process of interchange going on between them. It ought to bind them to Paul all the more closely in gratitude and love.

When we put verses 8 and 9 together with chapter 1 verses

8 and 9, we discover a fascinating thing. Under pressure but not crushed, says Paul in the present passage; at a loss, but not at our wits' end; persecuted but not abandoned; cast down but not destroyed. But when we read chapter 1 we discover that *at the time* it really felt as though he *was* being crushed, at his wits' end, abandoned and destroyed. It felt as though he had received the sentence of death. What he says here he says with the benefit of hindsight, but he hasn't forgotten that it didn't feel like that when it was going on. This passage is an enormous comfort to all those who are going through persecution, temptation, suffering, bereavement, tragedy and sorrow of every kind. It feels as though you are being crushed – of course it does. That's how it felt for Paul as well. But it may actually mean that you are living out the gospel. This is what being a servant of Jesus **Christ** is often like. It is a way of making sure that neither you nor anyone else mistakes the servant for the master, the envelope for the letter.

2 CORINTHIANS 4.13–18

The God of All Comfort

[13]We have the same spirit of faith as you see in what is written, 'I believed, and so I spoke.' We too believe, and so we speak, [14]because we know that the God who raised the Lord Jesus will raise us with Jesus and present us with you. [15]It's all because of you, you see! The aim is that, as grace abounds through the thanksgiving of more and more people, it will overflow to God's glory.

[16]For this reason we don't lose heart. Even if our outer humanity is decaying, our inner humanity is being renewed day by day. [17]This slight momentary trouble of ours is working to produce a weight of glory, passing and surpassing everything, lasting for ever; [18]for we don't look at the things that can be seen, but at the things that can't be seen. After all, the things

you can see are here today and gone tomorrow; but the things you can't see are everlasting.

'To Carthage then I came,' wrote T. S. Eliot in one of his famous poems. One can imagine someone picking up the poem in a bookshop and wondering what on earth he was talking about. Had he gone to the real Carthage, in North Africa? If so, what had that to do with the rest of the poem? Why did he go on to speak of 'Burning, burning'? And why did he then say, 'O Lord thou pluckest me out'? This is the kind of thing that makes some people despair of twentieth-century poetry.

But this kind of thing makes other people appreciate it all the more. Once you have discovered what Carthage means, not only does the rest fall into place; a whole world is conjured up, a world we can step into in our imagination, a world that provides a totally different dimension for the poem. Eliot is, in fact, alluding to one of the most famous writers, and one of the most famous books, in the early Western world: to St Augustine, and to his *Confessions*. Augustine describes how he went to Carthage as a young man, and found it to be a place where lust was stirred up and celebrated, a place from which only God himself could, and in Augustine's case did, 'pluck him out'. Eliot, using first one phrase, then another, invites us to think of modern equivalents of Carthage, and of the 'I' in the poem as a modern Augustine. One phrase contains a whole world.

Paul sometimes plays this trick, too, quoting a short line from the Bible when he wants his readers to imagine the whole setting and mood. This time the quotation itself is from a poem, the biblical poem we call Psalm 116. 'I believed, and so I spoke'; it doesn't sound very impressive, we feel, just like that, since after all most people who speak out on any given topic believe in what they're saying. But wait a minute. What's going on in the psalm as a whole? And what's going on in this passage in the letter? Do they fit together in some way?

They most certainly do. Paul has been talking on and off all the letter, and particularly in the last few verses, about the way in which he had found himself crushed and ready to die – and about the way in which, to his surprise, the power of God was able to raise him from that death and give him new **life**. That is what the psalm is all about:

¹I love **YHWH**, because he has heard my voice and my prayer; ²he has turned his ear towards me; so I will call on him throughout my whole life.

³The traps of death were around me; the pangs of the underworld grabbed me; I was troubled and bitter.

⁴Then I called on YHWH's name: 'YHWH,' I said, 'rescue my life!'

⁵YHWH is kind and just; our God is full of mercy.

⁶YHWH looks after the simple; when I was down in the depths, he rescued me.

⁷So, my heart, you can go back to rest; YHWH has been very generous to you.

⁸For you have rescued my life from death, my eyes from tears, and my feet from tripping up.

⁹I live my life in YHWH's presence, here in the land of living people.

¹⁰*I remained faithful, and so I spoke:*

'I'm in deep trouble,' I said.

¹¹I even said, like a fool in a hurry, 'Everyone is telling lies!'

¹²What can I do out of gratitude to YHWH, in return for all his kindness to me?

¹³I will take the cup of salvation, and call on YHWH's name.

¹⁴I will give back to YHWH what I promised I would, in front of all his people.

¹⁵When YHWH's people die, it is weighty and precious to him.

¹⁶I am your servant, YHWH; your servant, and your servant-girl's son; you have untied me and set me free.

¹⁷I will offer a thanksgiving-sacrifice to you, and call on YHWH's name.

¹⁸I will give back to YHWH what I promised I would, in front of all his people,

¹⁹In the courtyards of YHWH's house, in the middle of you, O Jerusalem –

YHWH be praised!

We hardly need to spell out the point: the psalm fits Paul's situation like a glove. You can see what he's done. Knowing the Bible as well as he did, and continuing as he had from boyhood to weave the psalms through his daily prayers, he found the experiences he had had in recent days fitting in uncannily well to what the Psalmist was talking about. The traps of death were around him, the bitter smell of the underworld seemed to be coming for him, dragging him down. And there, down in the depths, YHWH, Israel's God, came to his rescue; the God Paul now knew as the father of Jesus, the one by whose power the **Messiah** himself had gone down into death and been brought up to new life. So it was with him: 'You have rescued my life from death, my eyes from tears and my feet from tripping up.'

So, as he reflects here on the whole experience, he finds himself in the same position as the Psalmist in verse 10: he has stayed faithful, and so now speaks. The Psalmist stayed faithful, and spoke – to YHWH himself in desperate prayer, in the anguish of his heart, and to those who would read and sing his poem. Paul remains faithful, and speaks in prayer and thanksgiving to the God who raised the Lord Jesus. He speaks within his own heart, and now to those who read his letter:

because, as with the psalm, so Paul is keen that the end result would be more praise arising to the living God. The more people are praising God, the more the world is taking the shape it was meant to have, and the more God's power goes out to save and heal where those generous blessings are still needed. Paul has taken the whole psalm, has lived through its experience himself, has reflected deeply on it in the light of the **gospel** of Jesus, and has now made it the instrument of his appeal to the Corinthians not to despise his sufferings or regard him as a failure, but to share his gratitude to God and turn the whole experience into praise.

So he comes back in verse 16 to where he was at the start of the chapter: explaining why he doesn't lose heart despite the circumstances that might have made people think he had fallen out of God's care and purpose altogether. And, to back up this repeated assertion, he comes out with one of the most astonishing statements of Christian hope ever written.

Unfortunately, it's easy today for people to misunderstand it. It's easy to imagine, within the worldview that many have today, that in verses 17 and 18 he's saying that bodily things, outward things, don't matter. It is easy to assume that he's insisting on true reality being non-bodily things, 'spiritual' things in that sense. But, as his other writings, and indeed the next chapter, will make clear, this is not the case. He is talking not about 'physical' and 'non-physical' things, but about the *present* world as contrasted with the *future* world. The point about 'things you can see' is that they last for only a short while. But God's true reality, which will one day be brought to birth in his new world, is more richly physical in ways we can hardly imagine, though at present out of sight.

All we know about it is that it will involve 'a weight of glory'. The glory of the giving of the **law** was as nothing to the glory we already have in the gospel, as he argues in chapter 3. Now Paul declares that the glory we presently have, which is like treasure in earthenware pots (verse 6), is as nothing compared with the glory that is yet to be revealed. And in that light even the huge, overwhelming, deadly sorrows and difficulties that Paul had endured appeared as 'slight momentary trouble'. He had come to realize that the present body is only the beginning, the initial clothing for a true self that will one day be much more fully clothed. That is totally different from saying 'the present body is the outer shell for a true self which is non-bodily and will one day, thank God, be freed from the whole business of bodies'. It is more like saying: 'I live in a tent at present, but one day I shall live in a palace!'

That's precisely what Paul does go on to say in the next chapter. But for the moment we can note where this whole discussion has got to. Paul is still talking about his apostolic vocation and ministry, and explaining why, though his sufferings might look as though he should be losing heart, in fact he does not. In order to make this point he has now laid out almost a complete picture of the future **resurrection**, and how it relates to the present suffering. He will now go on to fill in this picture, and show where his ministry fits within God's entire project to reconcile the world to himself.

2 CORINTHIANS 5.1–5

A House Waiting in the Heavens

[1]For we know that if our earthly house, our present 'tent', is destroyed, we have a building from God, a house no human hands have built: it is everlasting, in the heavenly places. [2]At the present moment, you see, we are groaning, as we long to put on our heavenly building, [3]in the belief that by putting it on we won't turn out to be naked. [4]Yes: in the present 'tent', we groan under a great weight. But we don't want to put it off; we want to put on something else on top, so that what is doomed to die may be swallowed up with life. [5]It is God who has been

> at work in us to do this, the God who has given us the spirit as the first instalment and guarantee.

Life after death is one of the greatest mysteries in the world, but there's no need to make it more mysterious than it should be.

I recently went for the first time to the magnificent Sistine Chapel in the Vatican, beside St Peter's Church in Rome. There on the wall is the world-famous Michelangelo painting of the Last Judgment. I pondered it long and hard, considering the ways in which the scene it depicts was already thoroughly traditional by Michelangelo's day (the sixteenth century), and the way in which paintings like that, by him and many others, made sure that, whatever people said in the pulpit or wrote in books, the image of some people going off to '**heaven**' and others going down to '**hell**' remained firmly fixed in the imagination.

So firmly established is this picture, indeed, that if you try to suggest to people that it's misleading, they simply won't understand. They will imagine you are saying either that there is no afterlife at all, or that everyone goes to heaven irrespective of the life they have lived.

But in this passage – and it is typical of many in the New Testament – 'heaven' is not *the place we go to when we die*, but rather *the place where God has our future bodies already in store for us*. Paul uses two pictures to make this clearer.

First, he refers to the body as a 'house' or 'tent' (in his world, of course, many people lived in tents all the time, which was one of the reasons why there was always work for a tentmaker like him). This enables him to say both that the present body can be exchanged for a better one in due course, and that being embodied matters. Though the idea of a house or tent does allow him to think of the 'self' as losing one dwelling place and gaining another, it also suggests strongly that the point of the exercise is not to give up having a body altogether. Everybody needs to live somewhere.

He combines this with the idea of the body as 'clothing'. This enables him to say a similar thing from a slightly different angle: the Christian hope for the future is not about becoming *disembodied* but about being *re-embodied*. We don't, as he says, want to turn out to be 'naked', a bare **spirit** or **soul** without any 'clothing'. In fact, the hope he expresses in verse 4 is seen in terms of putting more clothes on, on top of the ones we're wearing already: we don't want to be *un*clothed, but to be *more fully* clothed. And the transformation he has in mind, exactly as in 1 Corinthians 15, is that whereas the present body is 'mortal', 'doomed to die', heading for corruption and decay whether we like it or not, the body that is to come will be full of life, a life that nothing can harm or destroy.

What then does he mean by speaking of this new body in the way he does in verse 1? The present version of the human body, he says in 1 Corinthians 15.47–49, is 'earthly', in the sense that it is made of earthly material, belongs on the present earth, and will eventually return to it. The new body, however, which in 1 Corinthians 15.44 and 46 he refers to as 'animated by the spirit', is waiting in heaven, in God's space and sphere, and it is of a kind which will never wear out. When he says it's 'not made with hands', he is using a regular Jewish phrase which contrasts something given or done by God himself with something that mere humans have produced.

The **resurrection** body, then, will be similar to the present one in some respects and quite different in others. It's hard to imagine just what it will be like; the resurrection of Jesus himself was regarded by Paul and others in the early church as the model and prototype of the one that is to come, but that doesn't tell us much except that it really is what we would call a body but with startling new properties. And Paul returns once more to what he said in 1.22: the **holy spirit**, God's own gift to all his people in the present time, is the first instalment and guarantee of the new life that is yet to come. The spirit, as Paul says in Romans 8.9–11, was the means by which God raised Jesus himself; and the spirit will do the same for us.

Paul's picture of wanting to put something extra on, not to take our present 'clothes' off, introduces a remarkable possibility. Why do almost all humans wear clothes, not only in cold climates where they need them to keep warm, but in very hot ones where they would be just as comfortable without? It isn't just 'shame', in the sense of modesty, though that's part of it. It certainly isn't 'shame' in the sense of 'guilt', though there are some cultures that have felt ashamed, in that sense, of the human body. No: if Paul is right, there is something deep down within every human being which knows that we are made for more than this. Clothes are an anticipation of our resurrection bodies. The reason we take trouble over them, insofar as we do, is not just pride or a desire to show off, though of course that may come into it as well. At a deeper level than that, it is because we know that we are, in the present, a shadow of the self God wants and intends us to be. Wearing clothes is a sign of that 'something more', that fuller existence which we glimpse but cannot, in this life, grasp and possess.

The reason Paul is saying all this is not simply that he wants the Corinthians to understand the resurrection hope (though of course he does, and the present passage is an important supplement to what he said in 1 Corinthians 15). It is, rather, that he wants them to understand that his present work as an **apostle**, though it carries death about with it, also carries, by the spirit, the sure hope of resurrection. Once they realize that, they may learn to see not only him, but their own selves, in quite a new light.

And the same applies to us, too.

2 CORINTHIANS 5.6–10

The Judgment Seat of the Messiah

[6]So we are always confident: we know that while we are at home in the body we are away from the Lord. [7]We live our lives by faith, you see, not by sight. [8]We are confident, and we would much prefer to be away from the body and at home with the Lord. [9]So we make it a point of honour to please him, whether we are at home or away. [10]For we must all appear before the judgment seat of the Messiah, so that each may receive what has been done through the body, whether good or bad.

The first thing we were shown when we went to Corinth was the judgment seat. You come up the road Paul would have walked, climbing a bit as you get to the middle of the town, and you find yourself standing in the ancient Forum, which would have been lined with shops, temples and public buildings. The most important of the public buildings, on the south side of the Forum, were the government headquarters; and there, in the middle, is the place where, in Paul's day, the Roman governor would sit to dispense justice, to try cases. The judgment seat. It's often referred to by its Greek term: the *bema*.

That, of course, is where Paul himself ended up on his first visit, according to Acts 18.12–17. (This, incidentally, helps us to date Paul's journeys, because the proconsul who heard the accusation and dismissed the case was one Gallio, a brother of the philosopher Seneca, and we know from an inscription that Gallio was in Corinth between AD 50 and 52.) In many modern societies, justice is dispensed behind closed doors. People see fictional trials on television, and, in some countries, actual trials broadcast on live television; but most people don't see the inside of a courtroom for themselves more than once or twice in their lives. In most ancient towns it wasn't like that.

Justice was very public. Everybody could see what was going on.

The picture Paul draws here is of everybody appearing before the *bema* of the **Messiah**. Everybody will be brought, so to speak, up the road into the centre of town, to stand before the Messiah and receive the reward for the things which they have done with their bodies, whether good or bad. This is one of the clearest statements of the last judgment in Paul's writings, and indeed anywhere in the New Testament.

I said in the previous section that some aspects of the great last judgment scenes painted by Michelangelo and others are misleading. In particular, the idea of 'going to **heaven**' as a final destination can trick people into imagining that the Christian teaching about what happens after death is that you leave the body behind and go off into a non-bodily state where the '**soul**' is either saved or lost. That is clearly wrong. Paul argues that we shall be given new bodies, not immediately after we die (unless the Lord returns then), but on the great day of **resurrection** which lies in the future. But this doesn't mean that there won't be a judgment. Here and elsewhere (for instance, Romans 2.1–16 and 14.10) Paul makes it very clear: there will come a time when every single human being will have to give an account of himself or herself.

This comes as a shock to many people today, and we must explain things a little further. But first, let's note how he describes our situation *between* the time of our death and the time of the final judgment. His picture of the resurrection of the body in verses 1–5 is not a picture of something that happens immediately after death, but of something that happens to enable us to stand before our Lord when he comes as judge. So what goes on in between?

Paul is quite clear. This, actually, is one of the points where the **gospel** enables him to be clearer than other Jewish teachers of the time. When he dies, he will be 'at home with the Lord'.

During this life, although we know the Lord Jesus by **faith**, not least when we share the fellowship of his sufferings (Philippians 3.8–10), we are essentially 'away from the Lord'. He is in heaven; we are on earth. At the moment heaven and earth, the two interlocking spheres of God's good creation, have not come together as, in God's eventual purpose, they will (Revelation 21), when, in answer to countless prayings of the Lord's own prayer, God's **kingdom** comes 'on earth as in heaven'. The central feature of that new world will be, of course, the personal and royal presence of Jesus himself at the centre of the new creation. But in the meantime, when they die, members of the royal family (those who have been 'anointed' by the **spirit**, as Jesus was: see 1.21) go from the body to be 'with the Lord'. There they will wait until the time when everything is made new. That's why Paul can speak in Philippians 1.23 of his desire 'to depart and be with the Messiah', which would be a glorious and welcome relief from his present sufferings.

That is why, too, we live our present lives, in the famous phrase, 'by faith, not by sight'. We need to be clear what this means.

Faith is the opposite of *sight*: it is hard, trusting day by day and believing things we don't see. People tell us we're stupid to go on believing them: where is the evidence, they ask? But if everything was obvious, or at least could be proved in some way, where would faith be? We must beware of any suggestion that the Christian faith gives us the kind of 'certainty' that people often crave. If I have that kind of certainty, I no longer need to trust God.

But faith is also the opposite of *doubt*. Some people today like to suggest that, since faith means believing things we don't see, it also means that we can't be sure about anything very much, so we have to put all kinds of things on hold, including our commitment to the hard-edged gospel itself, which declares that Jesus is indeed the world's true Lord, and that other gods and lords who claim that title are simply wrong. The present passage shows how mistaken this idea is. We live by faith, not sight; but that doesn't mean we don't believe that Jesus will come as judge.

This brings us back to the two questions people often ask about the last judgment.

First, isn't it odd that Paul, who elsewhere speaks of **justification** by faith, speaks here of doing our best to please the Lord, because one day we will stand before him to receive the reward or recompense for what we have done? How do we put together the different things he says?

The answer is that Paul always assumes, and often affirms, the reality of a future judgment which will be 'according to works'. But he also insists that when someone believes the gospel, confessing Jesus as Lord and believing that God raised him from the dead, *the future verdict is brought forward into the present*. This is the extraordinary thing about 'justification by faith', as we find it particularly in Romans and Galatians. 'Justification by faith' does *not* mean that God has decided that moral behaviour doesn't matter after all, and that the only thing that matters is something else, called 'faith', so that as long as I have this 'faith' it doesn't matter what I do. On the contrary. When Paul says that 'there is no condemnation for those in the Messiah' (Romans 8.1), he at once explains that this is because (a) God has condemned sin in the Messiah, so ultimate condemnation is impossible for those who are 'in him', and (b) God has given his spirit to the Messiah's people, and the spirit will enable them to become, in their moral behaviour, the people he has already declared them to be in justification. These are of course complicated matters, and we need a careful reading of Romans and Galatians to understand them fully. But it would be quite wrong to suggest that the idea of a last judgment according to present behaviour is ruled out by the gospel itself.

Second, people often suggest that since God is a God of love he will surely forgive everyone anyway. This gets near the heart of a major confusion of our times. *Forgiveness does not mean moral indifference*. If someone were to murder my best friend, it would be my difficult duty to forgive them; but that would not mean pretending it didn't matter, or that it hadn't been deeply hurtful, or that the living God does not hate such actions and will judge them. We mustn't mistake forgiveness for mere tolerance. God doesn't tolerate evil. He hates it. He will not allow it into his new creation. If he did, he would be an evil, foolish and unjust God. Paul believed, with the whole Jewish tradition behind him and the death and resurrection of Jesus before his gaze, that God was and is good, wise and just, and that one day the whole world will know it.

2 CORINTHIANS 5.11–15

The Messiah's Love Makes Us Press On

[11]So we know the fear of the Lord; and that's why we are persuading people – but we are open to God, and open as well, I hope, to your consciences. [12]We aren't trying to recommend ourselves again! We are giving you a chance to be proud of us, to have something to say to those who take pride in appearances rather than in people's hearts.

[13]If we are beside ourselves, you see, it's for God; and if we are in our right mind, it's for you. [14]For the Messiah's love makes us press on. We have come to the conviction that one died for all, and therefore all died. [15]And he died for all in order that those who live should live no longer for themselves, but for him who died and was raised on their behalf.

'What on earth made you do that?'

The newspaper reporter was incredulous. A young woman had just won a competition. The first prize was a three-week trip around the world. The chance of a lifetime. And she had given it up in order to stay with a friend as she went into hospital to face a crucial, and terrifying, operation.

'I mean,' went on the reporter, 'surely she'd have understood? There must have been other people who could have been with her?'

The young woman remained silent, pursing her lips. Eventually, seeing she wasn't going to get away with saying nothing, she burst out,

'All right. You really want to know. You think I'm crazy. But what none of you know – and I wasn't going to tell you – is what she did for me three years ago. I was on drugs and I couldn't stop. It got worse and worse. My family threw me out. She was the only person who looked after me. She sat up all night, again and again, and talked me through it. She mopped me down when I threw up, she changed my clothes, she took me to the hospital, she talked to the doctors, she made sure I was coming through it. She helped me with the court case. She even helped me get a job. She – she – she *loved me!* So did I have any choice? Now that she's sick herself, it's the least thing I can do to stay with her. That's far less than she did for me.'

The logic of love outweighs all other logic known to the human race. That sense, of a love which changes everything, and gives people the power to face things and do things they wouldn't otherwise have done, is what Paul is talking about in this passage. It becomes clear from the opening lines that he is still addressing the question: why, as an **apostle** of the **Messiah**, does he behave in the way he does? Why does he suffer so much? Why isn't he more like the sort of leaders and teachers that the Corinthians expected and wanted?

He has spoken in chapter 4 of the messianic pattern of dying and living which Jesus established and which he, Paul,

as an apostle of King Jesus, must follow. That alone is powerful enough. But he has then gone on to speak, in the earlier
part of this chapter, of the promise of a new **life**, a new body,
a new creation, in which all that is done here in this life will
find its fulfilment in a new dimension. And he has then spoken
of the judgment seat of the Messiah, before which all must
stand. However much he knows that there is 'no condemnation'
for those who belong to the Messiah (Romans 8.1), there is
still (as we saw in the previous section) the sense of terrible
responsibility as he thinks of the coming moment when he
will face the judge who knows the secrets of all hearts.

Therefore, he says (verse 11), we know the fear of the Lord;
not a cringing terror before an uncaring despot, but awe and
inadequacy before the incarnate Lord of all. This, too, should
help to explain why he does what he does; he isn't concerned
about what human standards people might impose from the
various cultures they live in, since the only standard that
matters is the one that Jesus himself will set. Facing that, he
says, he is open to God: God knows his sincerity and intentions. And he hopes the Corinthians will realize it too; then
they can hold their heads up when they think of him (verse
12), instead of judging him, and feeling ashamed of him as
their apostle, because they are thinking in purely human,
purely worldly terms.

But even this doesn't get to the heart of it, and so Paul makes
one further move which brings us into a different dimension
altogether. 'You really want to know,' he asks, 'why we behave
as we do? Are you still concerned that our style of life and
ministry is so different from what you might have expected?
Well, then,' (verse 13): 'I may sometimes seem as though I'm
out of my mind, but if that's the case it's because I'm working
for God, not for you! But sometimes I am deadly sober and
serious, and that's when I have to deal with you! But underneath it all is *the love of the Messiah*.' The underlying reason

why the apostle behaves as he does is not because of a theory, not because of fear of judgment, but because of love.

The Messiah has loved me, he says in Galatians 2.20, and given himself for me; nothing shall separate me from the Messiah's love (Romans 8.35). The Messiah's love gives me new energy, it urges me on, it impels me forward. That's what all love does: it constrains us, forces us to do things. If you want to be free from all constraints, learn to live without love! And the love of the Messiah is what the **gospel** is all about; the summary at the end of verse 15 looks straight across to the summary of the gospel itself in 1 Corinthians 15.3–4 ('the Messiah died for our sins . . . and was raised . . .'). The gospel is not just a mechanism for getting people saved. It is the announcement of a love that has changed the world, a love that therefore takes the people who find themselves loved like this and sends them off to live and work in a totally new way.

The energy to get up and go on as a Christian, as one who works for the gospel, therefore, comes not from a cold sense of duty, not from a fear of being punished if you don't do your bit, but from the warm-hearted response of love to the love which has reached out, reached down, and reached you. It may, of course, make you do things in ways that surprise or even shock other people. The gospels are full of that sort of thing; so is the story of Paul's life. But, as he now goes on to say, if a new world has come to birth, you wouldn't expect it to look exactly like the old one, would you?

2 CORINTHIANS 5.16—6.2

New Creation, New Ministry

[16]From this moment on, therefore, we don't regard anybody from a merely human point of view. Even if we once regarded the Messiah that way, we don't do so any longer. [17]Thus, if

anyone is in the Messiah, there is a new creation! Old things have gone, and look – everything has become new!

¹⁸It all comes from God. He reconciled us to himself through the Messiah, and he gave us the ministry of reconciliation. ¹⁹This is how it came about: God was reconciling the world to himself in the Messiah, not counting their transgressions against them, and entrusting us with the message of reconciliation. ²⁰So we are ambassadors, speaking on behalf of the Messiah, as though God were making his appeal through us. We implore people on the Messiah's behalf to be reconciled to God. ²¹The Messiah did not know sin, but God made him to be sin on our behalf, so that in him we might embody God's faithfulness to the covenant.

^{6.1}So, as we work together with God, we appeal to you in particular: when you accept God's grace, don't let it go to waste! ²This is what he says:

I listened to you when the time was right,
I came to your aid on the day of salvation.

Look! The right time is now! Look! The day of salvation is here!

When a new world is born, a new way of living goes with it.

This is true in so many stages of life. It is true when a couple have their first baby; a whole new chapter has opened in their lives, and nothing will be the same again. They have new responsibilities; everywhere they go, they see things with new eyes. It is true when people who have lived in a small and badly equipped house move into a large and well-appointed one. No more trips out of the back door to get running water. No more piles of washing in the living room armchairs. And it is true when people move from one country to another. A new language needs to be learnt. New laws apply. If you speak the old language, and live by the old laws, you won't fit in. You won't know what's happening.

But that, Paul implies, is what the Corinthians are still doing. He is still appealing to them to see the world with the new eyes of the **gospel**, instead of expecting everything, particularly his own style of apostleship, to conform to the fashions and customs of the world they were used to. The old world was a 'merely human' world. Paul uses one of his favourite phrases for this, which literally means 'according to the flesh'; but he doesn't mean 'flesh' as in 'physical body'. He means 'flesh' as in 'old, corruptible, passing away'. A new world has come about, through the death of Jesus in the 'flesh' in that sense, and the **resurrection** of Jesus in a new body, gloriously physical but not corruptible. The challenge of the gospel is to live cheerfully in that new world. Paul's challenge to the Corinthians is to recognize that that's what he's doing.

He begins by describing, in sweeping terms, the view from where he now is. He is on the threshold of the new creation itself, and everything looks different because everything *is* different. When he looks at other people, other Christians, himself, anyone, he sees them in a new way from how he did before. When he looks at the **Messiah**, he sees him, too, in a new way; there was a time when all his dreams of a Messiah were concentrated on 'purely human', that is, 'fleshly', ideals – a Messiah who would conquer the enemies of God, build the **Temple** of God, establish a 'purely human' kingdom. All such dreams must come to dust; that's what the Messiah's death and resurrection have taught him. The way to the true **kingdom** is *through* death, and out the other side into God's new world.

So: put together what he's learnt about other people and what he's learned about the Messiah, and what do you get? Verse 17, one of his great summaries of what Christianity is all about. In the Greek language he was using, he said it even more briefly: 'If anyone in Messiah, new creation!' The 'new creation' in question refers both to the person concerned and to the world which they enter, the world which has now been reconciled to the creator.

The next verses (18 and 19) explore this theme of reconciliation, emphasizing that what has happened in and through the Messiah is not a matter of God claiming a world that didn't belong to him, or making a new one out of nothing, but of God *reconciling* to himself his own world, his beautiful and beloved creation, after the long years of corruption and decay. And this, once more, explains what Paul is up to. If God was doing all this in the Messiah, that work now needed to be put into effect, to be implemented. The great symphony of reconciliation composed on Calvary needed to be copied out into orchestral parts for all the world to play. And that's where Paul and the other **apostles** come in. 'God was reconciling the world to himself in the Messiah, *and entrusting us with the message of reconciliation.*' He says it twice, in very similar words, to rub the message home. Something new *has* happened; something new *must now* happen. The world has never before seen a ministry of reconciliation; it has never before heard a message of reconciliation. No wonder the Corinthians found Paul's work hard to fathom. It didn't fit any preconceived ideas they may have had. He was behaving like someone . . . who lived in a whole new world.

This new world has a new king, and the king has ambassadors. Paul is not offering a new philosophy, though his message makes robust philosophical sense in its own way. He is not inviting people to try out a new religious experience, though anyone who believes his gospel will have experiences they had never imagined. He is going into all the world with a message from its newly enthroned sovereign, a message inviting anyone and everyone to be reconciled to the God who made them, loves them, and has provided the means of reconciliation for them to come back to know and love him in return. The second half of verse 20 isn't addressed to the

Corinthians in particular, as some translations imply; it's a general statement of Paul's ministry. He is saying, in effect, 'This is what I do! I'm not a philosophical teacher or rhetorical trickster; I'm a reconciler!'

The famous verse 21 is often misunderstood, too. It isn't a general statement about the meaning of the cross, though no doubt Paul would be happy to read it that way as well. It is a statement, as the whole of the last three chapters have been, about his own ministry. He has been called not just to speak about the fact that God has been faithful to the covenant; he is called to *embody* that faithfulness, to have it worked out, as he has been arguing in chapters 4 and 5, in his own 'death' and new life, in his own getting ready to stand before the Messiah's judgment seat, and above all in his own answering love and devotion to the Messiah who had loved him so much. The cross itself, in all its inexhaustible meaning, stands behind the ministry which Paul exercises, which he wants the Corinthians to understand.

But how is this possible? As he asked in 2.16, who is capable of being God's agent in this extraordinary work? The answer is in the cross, on which God made the sinless Messiah to 'be sin' on our behalf. All our sins, our failings, our inadequacies, were somehow dealt with there, so that we – the apostles, and all who are called to be 'ministers of reconciliation' – could embody in our own lives the faithfulness of God. No wonder the Corinthians found it difficult to grasp what Paul was up to, why his ministry took the shape it did. Nothing like this had ever been thought of in the world before.

But on this basis he turns to them in the first two verses of chapter 6 with a direct appeal, which comes to us as much as to them. You've accepted God's grace; don't let it go for nothing! Make the most of it! The new creation is already here. God is saying 'Yes!' to all the prophecies (1.20), and he's saying it right now. This is the day of salvation, the right time. Make the most of it.

2 CORINTHIANS 6.3–13

God's Servants at Work

[3]We put no obstacles in anybody's way, so that nobody will say abusive things about our ministry. [4]Instead, we recommend ourselves as God's servants: with much patience, with sufferings, difficulties, hardships, [5]beatings, imprisonments, riots, hard work, sleepless nights, going without food, [6]with purity, knowledge, great-heartedness, kindness, the holy spirit, genuine love, [7]by speaking the truth, by God's power, with weapons for God's faithful work in left and right hand alike, [8]through glory and shame, through slander and praise; as deceivers, and yet true; [9]as unknown, yet very well known; as dying, and look – we are alive; as punished, yet not killed; [10]as sad, yet always celebrating; as poor, yet bringing riches to many; as having nothing, yet possessing everything.

[11]We have been wide open in our speaking to you, my dear Corinthians! Our heart has been opened wide! [12]There are no restrictions at our end; the only restrictions are in your affection! [13]I'm speaking as though to children: you should open your hearts wide as well. That's fair enough, isn't it?

We sat by the table, both of us exhausted. In between us, an equally tired toddler in a high chair. We had been up half the night with him, and his mood was reflecting how we felt. He was grumpy and thoroughly uncooperative. He was refusing to open his mouth. But we knew we had to get him to eat some supper or he would be awake and demanding food in the middle of the night once more. And we both craved a full night's sleep.

Finally I could bear it no longer. I put back my head and yawned, long and wide. And of course the miracle happened.

He copied me, opening his mouth and looking at me. And my wife popped in the first spoonful of supper before he realized the game was up. Then, once he'd realized how good it was, he wanted more. Sighs of relief all round.

Paul is speaking, he says, as though to children (verse 13). He is inviting them to open their hearts as wide as he has opened his. They have been grumpy with him, refusing to acknowledge that his style of ministry is the genuine thing. They have wanted someone different – perhaps an actual person who is even now in Corinth, gathering support. And they have criticized Paul for not being the right sort, not doing the right things.

But now he opens his heart in a long burst of rhetoric. This is the sort of person I've been, he says. Why don't I let my hair down and tell you exactly how it's been for me! And off he goes on the splendid catalogue of what he's had to do and face over his years of relentless travel and proclamation. He wants them to do the same: to open their hearts to him in affection, to tell him what is really happening, not to put up smoke-screens, and to welcome him with equal vulnerability to that which he is showing in this passage.

Because vulnerability is the name of the game at this point, if it hasn't been already in Paul's remarkably frank admissions. He wouldn't get any marks with the smart set in Corinth for reminding them about his beatings and imprisonments, his times of great suffering and difficulty. With the hindsight of two thousand years, the list reads to us like a catalogue of virtues, but Paul must have known that he was pushing his luck, sailing close to the wind. This was exactly the sort of thing many of his readers did not want to hear. But he presses on, trying every trick in his own rhetorical book to break through the crust of indifference and make them see: this is what it means to follow a crucified **Messiah**! This is what it means to be an **apostle** of the world's true Lord!

The list is full of paradox, putting together things that clash like two musical notes crying out for resolution. These are the points at which the new creation of the **gospel** grinds against the old world like upper and lower millstones, with the apostle caught in the middle and feeling as if he's being crushed to powder. The list of hardships in verses 5 and 6 are balanced by the list of qualities in verses 7 and 8. How do you react to sufferings, difficulties, hardships? Most of us don't have to put up with beatings and imprisonments, and if we did we'd be unlikely (I fear) to respond with kindness and genuine love. Hard work and sleepless nights – well, sometimes we go through that, but most of us do it only in bursts, and then we take well-earned rests. There is no sign that Paul did that too often. The challenges, and his responses, went side by side: the challenges kept coming, and he went on speaking the truth, relying on God's power, using God's weapons rather than those which come most naturally to the human race.

This must have been particularly difficult when, as in verses 8, 9 and 10, he found not only physical dangers and challenges but the sneers and raised eyebrows (or whatever the equivalent was in his world) of so many of his hearers, inside the church as well as outside. Imagine yourself being shamed and slandered, taunted as a deceiver, ignored as if you weren't worth bothering about, surviving assassination attempts and fierce 'judicial' punishments. Paul draws the sting of each by balancing them out: glory, praise, truth, true fame, **resurrection life** bursting through in the present, escape.

The extraordinary balance of the passage reveals the mark of genuine Christian authenticity. Christians sometimes talk as if life were simply a matter of glory, of celebration, of the Lord providing all our needs and everything going forward without a hitch. Nobody actually lives like that all the time, of course, and the effort to go on believing it in the face of the evidence can produce a double life, with all the dangers of hypocrisy and shallowness. Equally, some people – including some Christians – react so forcibly to a grinning, shallow, falsely cheerful spirituality that they make out that everything is gloomy and filled with trouble, a constant round of difficulty and frustration. Christian maturity gets the balance right. It isn't so much a matter of a bit of this and a bit of that; it's a lot of both, and at the same time. And part of the task, not only of being a Christian, but of leading a Christian community, is to be able to grieve and celebrate at the same time, to share the pain and the joy of the world, and indeed the tears and the laughter of God.

2 CORINTHIANS 6.14—7.1

Don't Be Mis-Matched

[14]Don't be drawn into partnership with unbelievers. What kind of sharing can there be, after all, between justice and lawlessness? What partnership can there be between light and darkness? [15]What kind of harmony can the Messiah have with Beliar? What has a believer in common with an unbeliever? [16]What kind of agreement can there be between God's temple and idols? We are the temple of the living God, you see, just as God said:

I will live among them and walk about with them;
I will be their God, and they will be my people.
[17]So come out from the midst of them,
And separate yourselves, says the Lord;
No unclean thing must you touch.
Then I will receive you gladly,
[18]And I will be to you as a father,
And you will be to me as sons and daughters,
Says the Lord, the Almighty.

[7.1]So, my beloved people, with promises like these, let's make ourselves clean from everything that defiles us, outside and inside, and let's become completely holy in the fear of God.

Every time a new Bible translation comes out, it seems, one of the questions people ask about it is whether the language is 'inclusive'. When it mentions men, does it mention women as well? Does it imply that all Christians are basically male, with females assumed but not seen? Granted that the original languages in which the Bible was written often used a male or masculine word and intended to include females within that, how should we put that into good contemporary speech whether in English or in any other language?

Of course, every language has its problems and questions. Sensitive people will want to avoid offending others where possible – while people who are equally sensitive, but perhaps about different issues, will be anxious about forcing the Bible into a mould designed by current political and social fashions. Some will just shrug their shoulders and point out that you can't please all the people all the time.

Often when I've been translating the New Testament I have quite deliberately used language which refers equally to all the people concerned. When Paul speaks to a church, he often uses the word we might translate as 'my brothers'. But since he's usually talking to women as well as men, it's clearly appropriate for us to find some other way of saying it. I have frequently translated it as 'my dear family'. And so on.

In this passage, remarkably enough, we can see Paul himself doing something very similar. He is quoting from several Old Testament texts which emphasize the huge privilege that God's people have, precisely in being his people. And in one of them he is adapting a biblical promise, not to the people in general, but to the King – to the son who would be born to David, whom God would 'raise up', and to whom God would be a father.

The passage in question is 2 Samuel 7.12–14:

When your days are fulfilled, and you sleep with your
    fathers,
I will raise up your seed after you, one who will come
    from your own body,
And I will establish his kingdom.
He will build a house for my name, and I will establish
    the throne of his kingdom for ever.
I will be a father to him, and he shall be a son to me.

This passage was, in fact, a favourite quotation in the early church, highlighting the fact that the **Messiah**, the coming king from the line of David, would be God's own **son** in a special way. But Paul has made two crucial moves in re-reading the text. First, he has opened it up so that what was promised to the coming king is now promised to all God's people. Second, he has made it clear, in doing so, that the word 'sons' needs to have 'and daughters' added, in case anyone thought the promise was for men only, not for women as well (see Galatians 3.28).

Does this mean that Paul is simply playing around with the text, making it mean whatever he wants? Not at all. Remember what he said in chapter 1: all God's promises find their 'Yes' in the Messiah, the anointed one . . . because God has 'anointed' us too (1.20–21)! It is part of Paul's most basic understanding that what is true of the Messiah is true of all his people, and that this is expressed in the fact that God's people have all been 'anointed' with God's own **spirit**. That's why he can sometimes even use the word 'Messiah' to refer, not just to Jesus as an individual, but to Jesus-and-his-people together (e.g. 1 Corinthians 1.13, 12.12; Galatians 3.16). Paul may appear at first sight to be using the text to say something quite different, but as usual when we get down underneath we find a deep resonance between the original text and his own interpretation, based on his understanding of the way in which God's promises have come true in the Messiah.

The passage in 2 Samuel 7 goes on at once to warn David that God will treat his son, God's adopted son, precisely *as* a son. This will mean that God will bring him up quite strictly, disciplining him when he goes astray. Paul may have that in mind as well throughout this passage, which warns against presuming upon God's love as an excuse for corrupting the purity of the church's life. And verses 16–18 of the present passage echo several other Old Testament passages in which this same note is present. Verse 16: 'I will be their God, they will be my people'; that comes from Ezekiel 37.27, the great promise of restoration after **exile** seen in terms of **resurrection**. Verse 17: 'come out from them and be separate'; that comes from Isaiah 52.11, in the middle of the passage about God's coming **kingdom**, rescuing the exiles from Babylon, and leading on to the work of the Servant of the Lord who would die and rise again to accomplish God's purpose. And verse 18, as well as echoing 2 Samuel 7.14, also carries an echo of Jeremiah 31.9, where God promises once more that he will bring his people back from Babylon, because he is a father to Israel, and Ephraim (one part of Israel) is his firstborn.

These are not passages taken at random. Together they all say: in the Messiah, God has fulfilled his many promises, particularly his promises that he would bring his people back from exile. But the real exile was not the exile in Babylon; it was the exile of death itself. And through the Messiah's own death and resurrection this exile has been undone. It is now time for God's people to come home to him, home from the land of sin and death, home to the father who will receive them with open arms. Not for the first time in Paul, we hear in this passage echoes of Jesus' great parable of the Prodigal Son (Luke 15.11–32).

Once we understand what Paul is doing in quoting these Old Testament texts, we should be able to understand the appeal of this passage as a whole. This is how it works: if you really are the returned-from-exile people, the people for whom sin and death have been defeated, the people whom the living God has embraced as his own sons and daughters, then you must look around at the pagan world, learn to see it as it really is, and take action appropriately. Paul does not want them to hide from the world, to live in secret; he's already made that clear in 1 Corinthians 5.9–10. But he doesn't want them to enter into close partnerships with those who are still living by the old way of life, which is in fact the way of death. In verses 14–16 he lines up the contrasts: you stand for justice, light, the Messiah, faithfulness, and the temple of God, whereas the world that rejects the gospel ultimately stands for injustice, darkness, Beliar (a rare word for the **satan**), unfaithfulness and idolatry. You must therefore take care to keep yourselves pure, not to let the world drag you down or force you into its own way (7.1).

The basic command, in 6.14, could refer to any sort of partnership, such as in business. But its most obvious reference is to marriage. In 1 Corinthians 7.12–16 Paul addresses the question of people who become Christians when their spouse does not, and tells them not to separate unless the unbelieving spouse wants to. But in verse 39 of that same chapter he makes it clear that when contracting a fresh marriage it is important that this be only 'in the Lord', in other words, to a fellow-Christian. That is the thrust of this passage as well.

Paul had no doubt witnessed the tensions and problems that arose when one partner came to belong to the Lord, with all that that meant, and the other one remained unbelieving. Anyone who thinks this doesn't matter very much, Paul would say, has simply not realized how serious belonging to the Messiah really is. If you have received privileges such as the ones he lists here, you mustn't trample on them as though they were worthless. That would be like the Prodigal Son spurning his father's welcome and going back to feed the pigs.

2 CORINTHIANS 7.2–10

The God Who Comforts the Downcast

[2]Make room for us! We haven't wronged anybody, we haven't ruined anybody, we haven't taken advantage of anybody. [3]I'm not saying this to pass judgment against you; I've already said that you are in our hearts, to die together and to live together. [4]I speak of you freely and often; I regularly boast about you; I am full of comfort, and fuller still of joy, over and above all our trouble.

[5]You see, even when we arrived in Macedonia, we couldn't relax or rest. We were troubled in every way; there were battles outside and fears inside. [6]But the God who comforts the downcast comforted us by the arrival of Titus, [7]and not only by his arrival but in the comfort he brought to us, by telling us about your longing for us, your lamenting, and your enthusiasm for me personally.

As a result, I was more inclined to celebrate; [8]because, if I did make you sad by my letter, I don't regret it; and, if I did regret it, it was because I saw that I made you sad for a while by what I had written. [9]Anyway, I'm celebrating now, not because you were saddened, but because your sadness brought you to repentance. It was a sadness from God, you see, and it did you no harm at all on our account; [10]because God's way of sadness is designed to produce a repentance which leads to salvation, and there's nothing to regret there! But the world's way of sadness produces death.

What is your image of what a successful Christian ought to look like? Do you have in the back of your mind a picture of a person who goes through life in perfect **faith** and trust, obedient to God in everything, never afraid of what may lie in wait around the next corner, always rejoicing even in adversity?

Do you find this image a bit depressing sometimes? It seems so unreal, so unlike not only our own lives but those of all the people we know well. Of course there are moments of joy, or celebration, of faith, of hope and of love. (At least, I hope there are.) But the course of Christian living doesn't run smoothly, and we all know it.

So where does the popular image of a 'successful Christian' come from? Well, some might say, from the New Testament. Doesn't Paul himself tell us to rejoice all the time, to praise God without ceasing, to give thanks in everything? Doesn't he say, in a famous passage in Philippians 4, that we should 'have no anxiety about anything', but should commit it all to God?

Yes, he does. But such comments need to be balanced out with the deeply personal and revealing passages like the present one. If you want to know what it looks like and feels like to have no anxiety about anything, committing it all to God, come with Paul as he struggles along the road, exhausted and emotionally drained after his terrible experiences in Ephesus. He goes north to Troas, then across the narrow strip of water between Asia and Europe, the waterway we call the Dardanelles and he called the Hellespont, and on through Macedonia. With every step of the way he was praying and hoping, but it was a constant tussle against fears that welled up inside and opposition that attacked him all around. Every day when he didn't find Titus waiting for him was another disappointment; every day he went on, hoping for good news but bracing himself for the worst. 'Having no anxiety about anything', as far as Paul was concerned, wasn't a matter of attaining some kind of philosophically detached state where he simply didn't care. He cared, and cared passionately. I think 'having no anxiety' meant, for him, taking every day's anxieties and, with a huge struggle and effort, dumping them on the God in whom he doggedly believed.

The description in verse 5 of his own mental state – and the physical state which went with it, as so often the body reflects what's going on in the mind – is a great antidote to any superficial or glib statement of what a normal Christian life is like. Thank God it's not always like this; there are times when everything is going much better. But thank God that Paul, too, not just people we'd be tempted to think of as second-rate, went through periods like this, where he couldn't get any rest, and found trouble and fear inside and out. Thank God both for the time before Titus arrived, when Paul faced despair and was able to speak of it, and for the time when Titus did arrive at last, bringing good news which Paul obviously found so refreshing that we can feel his sigh of relief as he writes this paragraph.

The journey through Macedonia, to the point where Titus, coming north from Corinth, finally met up with Paul, may explain the rather jerky sequence of paragraphs at this point in the letter. The one we've just looked at (6.14—7.1), with its command not to become 'yoked together' with unbelievers, seems to break in on the appeal he makes in 6.11–13, which he picks up again in 7.2–3. Then the next chapters, 8 and 9, seem much calmer, before the mood changes again, becoming more combative and provocative, in chapters 10—13. It may well be that Paul dictated the letter in bits as he was on the road, stopping night after night in different places. It may even be that some parts have become dislocated, and actually belong elsewhere. In particular, it's possible that 6.14—7.1, the last passage we looked at, is actually the 'painful letter', or part of it, to which he refers in 7.8 and 2.2–4; it would not be unknown in Paul's world for one document that made reference to another one to include the second one, conveniently, within it when it was copied out again. It's possible that whoever first made an edition of all Paul's letters included the earlier, somewhat sharper, letter at this point.

We can never be sure of that; but what we can be sure of is that Paul, writing eagerly back to the Corinthians after Titus has brought news from them, is concerned now that they should know how much he is eagerly longing to see them, and that he has no intention of being cross or harsh when he gets there. The tables have, it seems, been turned; Paul was anxious that the Corinthians were cross with him, ready to rebel against his authority, and now Titus has made it clear that *they* are anxious about what state of mind *he* will be in when he arrives, worried that he is going to be angry with them. So he wants to assure them not only that he has been greatly comforted by news of them, but that the sorrow they felt at what had passed between them was itself an excellent thing. All of which leads him to some profound and important reflections on two different types of sadness. There is God's way of sadness and there is the world's way of sadness, and there is all the difference you can imagine between the two.

What is the difference between God's way of sadness and the world's way of sadness? The two types can be seen sharply set out in two of the central characters of the **gospel** story. On the night of the Last Supper, Peter followed Jesus to the **high priest**'s house, where he proceeded to deny three times that he'd ever known Jesus. On realizing what he'd done, Peter went out and cried like a baby. That was the first step towards the restoration that came with Jesus' appearance to him (Luke 24.34; 1 Corinthians 15.5) and the remarkable conversation with Jesus by the lakeshore (John 21.15–19). His sadness led him to **repentance**, and that was a cause, ultimately, for rejoicing. On the other hand, Judas, who had betrayed Jesus, showing the high priest's servants where to find him in the dark, was plunged into the darker depths of the world's way of sadness. In Matthew's account, he flings down the money he'd been paid at the feet of the chief priests, and goes off and hangs himself (Matthew 27.5). Two types of sadness; two end results.

Paul is delighted and relieved that the sadness he'd caused by his letter has not resulted in the dark, closed mind so shockingly exemplified by Judas, but in the sorrow and repentance we associate with Peter. The Corinthians had been stung by his rebuke, but their sorrow had led them to see that they really should shape up and put their common life into order. They couldn't be proud any longer of the behaviour which they had tolerated in their midst (Paul may be referring to the incident of 1 Corinthians 5.1–5). They had to repent of it and put it right.

What has this passage done to our vision of normal Christian life? The answer, I hope, is that it has taken it right away from the smooth, easy picture of so much popular imagination, and has placed it alongside Paul as he goes through the strong and sudden mood swings of his journey through Macedonia; and, as well, alongside the Corinthians as they come to terms with unexpected and painful rebuke, plunging them into sadness which leads to repentance and making amends. Together Paul and Corinth make up a far more 'normal Christian life' than the standard, and almost wholly imaginary, picture. Let us not be afraid to journey with Paul, or to find ourselves in Corinth facing rebuke, knowing both God's way of sorrow and the joy of restoration.

2 CORINTHIANS 7.11–16

Our Boasting Proved True!

[11]Just look and see what effect God's way of sadness has had among you! It's produced eagerness, explanations, indignation, fear, longing, keenness, and punishment. You have shown yourselves faultless in the whole business. [12]So if I'm writing to you, it's not because of the person who's done the wrong, nor

because of the people who were wronged, but so that you can recognize for yourselves, in God's presence, just how eager you really have been for us. [13]We have been comforted by all of this.

The real celebration, though, on top of all our comfort, came because Titus was so overjoyed. You really did cheer him up and set his mind at rest. [14]I wasn't ashamed of the various boasts I had made to him about you. Just as I had always spoken the truth to you, so our boast to Titus turned out to be true as well. [15]He is constantly yearning for you deeply as he remembers the obedience you showed, all of you, and how you welcomed him with fear and trembling. [16]I am celebrating the fact that I have confidence in you in everything.

The first time I stayed with my friends in Germany I explained to them just how beautiful the north of England was. They had never seen it, and they had only heard a little about the hills and woods, the mountains, the ancient castles and the beautiful beaches. I was eager to tell them how many lovely places there were for a holiday or a visit. Most tourists who visit England come to see London; many then go on to Oxford and Cambridge, and particularly Stratford-on-Avon, where William Shakespeare was born. A much smaller number go to the north of the country and discover for themselves its softer, wilder delights. I was enthusiastic in my boasting about it to my friends.

To my surprise, and (I confess) rather to my alarm, they took me at my word, and promptly booked themselves a vacation in the far north of England for the following year. Of course, I told them how delighted I was. But secretly I was waiting anxiously. Would they find the best parts? Would it rain all the time? Would they think I had been exaggerating?

Fortunately the vacation was a great success. As far as I can tell (they may of course have been too kind to tell me the truth), they loved the place and the people, as most visitors do. I was relieved; my boasting had proved true.

That's the feeling Paul has had, now that Titus has come back from Corinth and told him that the Christians there are indeed as eager to get back on good terms with him as he is to do so with them. Anyone who has been involved in a relationship that has hit a sudden stormy patch, and has made overtures towards reconciliation, will know what that felt like.

Paul sees this vindication of his boasting to Titus as another sign that God is underscoring his general truthfulness. He hasn't been playing around with the **gospel**, with God's **word** (see 4.2), or with what he says to his associates about the work of God in the various churches. He has no vested interest in making up pretty lies to gain a good reputation. His only interest is in the truth. We today have learned, the hard way, to be cynical about such claims. Many feel cynical today when they read Paul. But that cynicism ought to be silenced by the situation Paul is now in. He is coming to see them, coming very soon now; and all will be revealed. There will be no hiding. Paul is not looking for false comfort, though goodness knows he could have done with any comfort he could get in the weeks and months leading up to the writing of this letter. He is looking for, and finding, true comfort in the only place it can be found: in the truth itself, the truth of God, the truth of the gospel, the truth of what the **holy spirit** is accomplishing in people's hearts and lives.

That, too, is why he now writes to them. In congratulating them on the range of emotions and activities that his letter had provoked in them, he is now writing to make it clear just how eager . . . they are for him. Verse 12, which says this, sounds odd when we first read it. If I write a letter to someone very dear to me, surely I'm more likely to tell them how fond *I* am of *them*, not how fond they are of me? Why does Paul need to tell the Corinthians how keen *they* are on *him*?

Paul has realized that the Corinthians have got themselves in quite a muddle. Not only have they been strongly influenced by teachers who have been pulling their minds and imaginations back to the prevailing culture and its standards and away from the **Christ**-shaped way of **life** that the gospel is meant to produce. They have been muddled about their allegiance to Paul himself: have they really offended him? Will he ever come back and embrace them, love them and look after them as he did before? Paul now needs to hold up a mirror to the Corinthians, and, perhaps with gentle humour, invite them to look into it. Are you worried, he seems to be saying, that your response to my sharp letter isn't good enough? Let me tell you what Titus has discovered: that you have responded in every way possible, getting your act together and sorting things out, like people spring-cleaning a house before a royal visit. Paul needs to assure them not only that he is much comforted, but that they are on the right track.

In particular, he wants to assure them, as he did in chapter 2, that they have acted properly in relation to the matter of discipline which had caused the problem in the first place. (I wonder how many Christians, when teetering on the brink of some sin, think of the problems they will cause, not only for themselves and any other people immediately involved, but for the whole church as it faces the question of how to deal with that sin? Not many, I fear; which may be a sign, not only that Christians are careless about the effects of their sin, but that the church is by no means always eager to exercise appropriate discipline.)

The letter has thus come round to a point of equilibrium. Paul has been through trouble and sorrow, fear and anxiety, acting out multiple forms of the dying of his Lord (see 4.10–12). Now, not simply through the work of the spirit in his own heart, but through the work of Titus in going to Corinth and bringing back the good news, he is greatly comforted, for which he thanks God from the bottom of his heart. This has brought his relationship with the Corinthians back to where it should be, and he is ready to proceed with the business he has to put to them. After all that has been said in the last few chapters, if they are not ready now to hear the appeal of chapters 8 and 9, they will never be.

2 CORINTHIANS 8.1–7

The Generosity of the Macedonian Churches

[1]Let me tell you, my dear family, about the grace which God has given to the Macedonian churches. [2]They have been sorely tested by suffering. But the abundance of grace which was given to them, and the depths of poverty they have endured, have overflowed in a wealth of sincere goodness on their part. [3]I bear them witness that of their own accord, up to their ability and even beyond their ability, [4]they begged us eagerly to let them have the privilege of sharing in the work of service for God's people. [5]They didn't just do what we had hoped; they gave themselves, first to the Lord, and then to us as God willed it. [6]This put us in a position where we could encourage Titus that he should complete this work of grace that he had begun among you. [7]You have plenty of everything, after all – plenty of faith, and speech, and knowledge, and all kinds of eagerness, and plenty of love coming from us to you; so why not have plenty of this grace too?

A magazine in Britain has a regular cartoon feature entitled 'Scenes You Don't Often See'. It's a sharp little comment on the selfishness of modern life, and has included drawings of such unlikely scenes as someone buying *two* copies of the magazine sold on the street by homeless people, or of a teenager in a railway carriage turning off his personal stereo in case it annoyed the people sitting next to him. We smile, because we wish people were like that – maybe we wish that *we* were like that! – and we know that, in normal life, they aren't and we aren't.

Some years ago I heard of a church (I'm not making this up) where the pastor once got into the pulpit to give his people a severe lecture about the level of giving in the church; not because they weren't giving enough but because *they were giving far too much*. He knew that most of his people weren't well off. He knew that the amount of money that had been coming in was way beyond what most of them could afford. He was genuinely worried that they were pushing themselves to the point of serious personal problems in order to support the work of the church.

'Scenes you don't often see'? Alas, yes. Mostly when pastors get into the pulpit to talk about giving money they do so with a heavy heart because yet again they have to point out that people aren't giving enough. But, as this passage indicates, simply urging people to give more isn't the whole story. In fact, it's not really what the story is about at all. In principle, the story is about what God is doing in the life of the church and congregation.

In this chapter and the next one Paul is walking on eggshells, yet he somehow gets away with it. His overall purpose is to make sure that by the time he arrives in Corinth the church will have put aside the full amount of money they are going to contribute for the impoverished Jerusalem church. He wrote about this briefly in the earlier letter (1 Corinthians 16.1–4), and despite the agony that has come about in the relationship between him and the church in the intervening period he is now determined to press ahead and complete the task. He doesn't just want to be fully and delightfully reconciled to the Corinthians. He wants them to share in the great project he has in hand: demonstrating to the Gentile churches that they are part of the same family as the Jewish Christians in Jerusalem, and, still more important, demonstrating to the Jerusalem Christians that those strange, uncircumcised **Gentiles** who, like them, have come to believe in Jesus the

Messiah are fellow members with them in God's renewed people, the family defined by their **faith** in the risen Jesus as Lord.

We might have thought that he was pushing his luck, trying to carry on with this project after all that has passed between him and Corinth; but he will not be deterred. He is desperately concerned for the unity of the whole Christian family, and he has glimpsed, as part of his missionary vocation, the possibility of doing something so striking, so remarkable, so practical that it will establish a benchmark for generations to come, a sign that Jewish Christians and Gentile Christians really do belong together.

And perhaps we shouldn't be surprised that, with a project like this on hand, he has run into huge personal difficulties and enormous tensions. When God's work is going ahead, dark forces will do their best to thwart or undermine it, as he admits at the next stage of the project (Romans 16.25–32; at verse 31 he asks the Roman church to pray that the collection will be 'acceptable' to the Jerusalem church, since he knows they may well be inclined to turn up their noses at money coming from non-Jewish sources). So he knows that at every stage the project is a tricky one: persuading the Gentile churches to hand over money, especially the Corinthian church that had seemed to rebel against him; taking the money safely, and with proper accounting, to Jerusalem; and delivering it acceptably to the church there.

This sense that he is treading very dangerously can be seen in the remarkable fact that in the whole of these two chapters he never once uses any of the Greek words for 'money' itself. He phrases everything very indirectly. But this isn't just because he's embarrassed about it, though it's possible that he may have been. The question of his financial relationship with Corinth, where he had consistently refused payment for his work as an **apostle**, had always been something of a sore point

(1 Corinthians 9.1–18; 2 Corinthians 11.7–11). They were puzzled, perhaps even offended, that he hadn't accepted money for himself; what will they now think when he asks for money at last, but supposedly for someone else? All kinds of difficulties and wrong impressions suggest themselves. So Paul phrases his entire appeal, not in terms of money as such, but in terms of *grace*.

Grace is one of Paul's 'big' words – so big, in fact, that we often fail to realize all the tasks he gets it to perform. Often when people talk about 'grace' in church circles they are referring simply to the undeserved love and power which God showers on people in bringing them to faith in the first place and enabling them to live and grow as Christians. That remains central and vital. But Paul also uses the word in what seems to us (though probably not to him) a different way, as in this passage: to refer to what God wants to do not just *in* and *for* Christians but *through* them. What does it mean that God gave 'this grace' to the churches in Macedonia (Philippi, Thessalonica, and perhaps some others)? It didn't simply mean they had what we would call a wonderful spiritual experience. It meant that, under an impulse which came from God himself, they gave money with almost reckless generosity. They were like the congregation whose pastor had to warn them that they were giving far too much. They were desperately poor, and had suffered serious persecution; these two things may have gone together, since the persecution may have included loss of jobs and income for some. But such was their devotion to God, to the Lord Jesus, to Paul himself, and to the work of the **gospel** and of church unity, that they found it in their hearts to give not only according to their means but way beyond. This, Paul declares, can only be a work of grace.

So, he declares, don't you want this grace as well? There is a gently teasing element to this, as verse 7 makes clear. The Corinthians were proud, as we have seen in this letter and the previous one, of their various spiritual attainments, the remarkable things that God had done and was doing in their lives. Well, he says, why not have a good helping of this grace as well? Complete your set of spiritual accomplishments: allow this work of grace, which Titus has already begun, to come to completion. (Titus had obviously been urging them to do what Paul had told them to in 1 Corinthians 16.1–4.)

It is a bold appeal. I have tried to imagine myself standing in front of a congregation and saying something like this, and I confess I find it difficult. But Paul knows, and those who have the God-given task of raising funds for the work of the gospel should never forget it, that what counts is not whipping up human sympathy for a project, nor making people feel guilty that they have money which others need, nor yet encouraging them to gain social prestige by letting it be known that they have given generously. What counts is a work of grace in the hearts and lives of ordinary people. Paul has seen this spectacularly in Macedonia; now he declares that he wants to see it in Corinth as well. Wouldn't he like to see it in the twenty-first-century church, too?

2 CORINTHIANS 8.8–15

Copying the Generosity of the Lord Jesus

[8]I'm not saying this as though I was issuing an order. It's a matter of putting their enthusiasm and your own love side by side, and making sure you genuinely pass the test. [9]For you know the grace of our Lord, King Jesus: he was rich, but because of you he became poor, so that by his poverty you might become rich. [10]Let me give my serious advice on this: you began to be keen on this idea, and to start putting it into practice, a whole year ago; it will now be greatly to your advantage [11]to complete your performance of it. If you do so, your finishing the job as far as you are able will be on the same scale

as your eagerness in wanting to do it. [12]If the eagerness is there, you see, the deed is acceptable, according to what you have, not according to what you don't have. [13]The point is not, after all, that others should get off lightly and you be made to suffer, but rather that there should be equality. [14]At the present time your abundance can contribute to their lack, so that their abundance can contribute to your lack. That's what makes for equality, [15]just as the Bible says: 'The one who had much had nothing to spare, and the one who had little didn't go short.'

A few months ago there was a news item about a woman crossing the Atlantic Ocean single-handedly in a rowing boat. At least, she ended up doing it single-handedly; to begin with, her husband had been with her, but he had become exhausted and totally demoralized, and he was flown back home while she battled on all by herself. The newspapers showed maps of how far they had got at the point where the husband left: about one-third of the way across.

Initial enthusiasm is not enough. There are many projects which seem exciting, a wonderful challenge, a chance to do something different and worthwhile. We set off eagerly to begin the work. But with almost everything worthwhile there comes a moment when the initial energy has drained away; the novelty of the project has worn off; and you have to make up your mind to go on despite the fact that at the moment it isn't any fun any more. (I hasten to add that I wouldn't dream of rowing a boat across the English Channel, let alone the Atlantic Ocean.)

But if you give up the project at the point where the initial energy and enthusiasm have run out, you will again and again be left with the frustrating sight of half-finished work. You were going to learn to play the violin, but there it is in its case in the attic because you never practised properly, and eventually gave up the lessons. You were going to write a novel, but the three chapters you wrote are sitting in the bottom drawer of the desk, and with every passing week you feel less and less like getting them out and starting again. You were going to transform the garden, and grow roses in one half and vegetables in the other; but you only dug half of it, and the few roses and potatoes that are struggling to get established make a mockery of what you had hoped it would look like. People often say they are looking for a new challenge, but often what that means is that they aren't prepared to face the real challenge of staying where they are, working through the present tiredness and boredom, and completing the job they have started.

That's how it is with Paul and Corinth. They made a start, but now they have to go on and finish the job. Presumably this means that they began, as Paul had earlier instructed them, to set aside money every Sunday, so that a fund would gradually build up which could be taken all at once to Jerusalem. Then, it seems, with the cooling of relations between Paul and the church in Corinth, they may just have stopped doing it. (This reminds us, of course, that someone must have been in charge of looking after the money in the meantime, accounting for it, and so on; these tasks are a deadly serious part of the work of the **gospel**.) Now, Paul says, don't leave the job half done! Complete what you started!

But the sense of not leaving a job half done isn't the deepest motivation he calls upon. At the centre of this passage, as of all Paul's thought, there lies not simply an obligation to other people, but the beating heart of the gospel itself: the death and **resurrection** of Jesus, the Lord, the **Messiah**. Verse 9 has been made famous through a well-known Christmas hymn written by F. Houghton:

Thou who wast rich beyond all splendour
All for love's sake becamest poor.

It sometimes surprises people, when they wonder where that idea came from, that it isn't in a great passage about the heights and depths of incarnational theology, discussing in wonderful detail all the complex questions about how Jesus can be both God and man, but instead in a passage which is basically saying 'Isn't it time you finished taking the collection?' And yet, on second thoughts, perhaps this passage *is* about the heights and depths of incarnational theology; because if theology is truly incarnational, truly about the way in which the eternal God took human flesh, and lived and died as one of us, the best way of expressing this is not in flights of abstract theory, leaving us with a nice set of well-organized ideas and beliefs, but in the practical, down-to-earth and often messy details of ordinary life, with its arrangements that go wrong and have to be put right, its plans that get left half-finished and have to be completed after the initial energy has run out, its personal relationships that go sour and have to find reconciliation. Perhaps, after all, these 'practical' chapters about money are among Paul's greatest *theological* writing . . .

And certainly verse 9 is drawing on the entire sweep of thought about who Jesus really was, and what he had achieved, which Paul can set out in much more detail in other passages. It reads, in fact, quite like a summary of the poem in Philippians 2.6–11, in which Jesus the Messiah does not regard his equality with God as something to exploit for his own advantage, but sees it as committing him to becoming human, becoming God's servant, and dying the terrible death of the cross. That's what Paul is referring to here: Jesus, with all the 'riches' of his life in the glorious mystery of God's inner being, became 'poor', both in the sense that becoming human was an astonishingly humbling thing and in the sense that the human life he took on was not royal, rich and splendid in the world's terms but instead poor, humble and eventually shameful. Paul has modelled his entire life and work on this Jesus, and he longs, throughout this letter, that the Corinthians will do so as well.

He has spoken of this from several angles, not least in chapter 4. Now, dealing with a specific and very practical question, he speaks of it again. Jesus did not lose heart halfway through the job. He was obedient 'even to death, yes, even the death of the cross'. That is what gives Paul heart in organizing this collection. When Jesus, for the sake of us all, became poor, we became rich; now, when people who follow him are ready to put their resources at his disposal, the world and the church may benefit, not only from the actual money but from the fact that when the Jesus-pattern of dying and rising, of riches-to-poverty-to-riches, is acted out, the power of the gospel is let loose afresh in the world, and the results will be incalculable.

Not that Paul intends anyone to become destitute as a result of the collection. He doesn't want to make the Corinthian Christians poor in order to make the Jerusalem ones rich! In Exodus 16.18, which he quotes in verse 15, God provided the 'manna', the bread from **heaven**, for the Israelites to eat; and there was enough (but not to spare) for each family and individual. Paul isn't just quoting the passage as a way of saying 'everyone will have what they need'. As so often, he is taking their minds back to the **Exodus** story which they, as God's renewed and redeemed people, are following in sequence, as they travel through the present life and world towards their promised inheritance. Paul is grounding his urgent appeal for generous giving both on the 'grace' of the Lord Jesus and on the underlying purpose of God, which is to ensure that his people do not go hungry on their journey home.

2 CORINTHIANS 8.16–24

Paul's Companions Are on Their Way

¹⁶But God be thanked, since he put the same eagerness for you into Titus's heart. ¹⁷He welcomed the appeal we made, and of his own accord he was all the more eager to come to you. ¹⁸We

have sent along with him the brother who is famous through all the churches because of his work for the gospel. [19]Not only so, but he was formally chosen by the churches to be our travelling companion as we engage in this work of grace, both for the Lord's own glory and to show our own good faith. [20]We are trying to avoid the possibility that anyone would make unpleasant accusations about this splendid gift which we are administering. [21]We are thinking ahead, you see, about what will look best, not only to the Lord, but to everybody else as well.

[22]Anyway, along with the two of them we are sending our brother, who has proved to us how eager and enthusiastic he is in many situations and on many occasions; he now seems all the more eager because he is convinced about you. [23]If there's any question about Titus, he is my partner, and a fellow worker for you. As for our brothers, they are messengers of the churches, the Messiah's glory. [24]So please give them a fine demonstration of your love, and of our boasting about you! Show all the churches that you mean business!

The smart white van pulled up outside the college one afternoon, and two men got out. Three or four students were in the common room, watching television. The men, wearing white coats like technicians, walked into the college and went into the common room. They went over to the large television.

'Sorry,' they said to the students. 'Needs replacing. Something not quite right.'

And with that they unplugged the television, picked it up, and walked out to the van.

The students shrugged, and accepted it as a fact of life. It was some while before they realized that something was indeed not quite right – but not with the television. The men were simply thieves, of a particularly bold variety.

Whenever anybody turns up out of the blue, previously unknown, we are naturally cautious – especially if they appear to have an interest in our property. I once walked, unannounced, into a shop belonging to a distant cousin in central Canada; he rightly quizzed me closely about the family history before being satisfied that I was genuine, and wasn't simply a trickster trying to get something for nothing. That is the kind of problem Paul is facing, and doing his best to head off. He is sending Titus back to Corinth (Titus must by now be feeling he knows the road up and down Greece rather better than he had expected), so that he can bring this letter to them and encourage them to get ready for Paul's own arrival. But – partly, no doubt, in case anyone should imagine that Titus was not to be trusted – he is also sending two other Christians, probably from the churches in Macedonia.

It's frustrating that Paul doesn't name these other two 'brothers'. We'd like to know who they were; we'd also like to know why Paul has decided to refer to them in this oblique, anonymous fashion. When Acts describes Paul's journey from Corinth after the visit he's now preparing for, it lists seven companions (Acts 20.4) – but not including Titus. Somehow we never have quite enough information to complete the jigsaw, to find out which companions went where when. But at least we know what is on Paul's mind as he writes this passage. He doesn't want the Corinthians to be in any doubt: these three, Titus and the two others, are genuine, bona fide workers for the **gospel**, and they are to be trusted completely. They are not in any way, shape or form, out for their own interests, encouraging the Corinthians to give money so that they can have some of it for themselves.

On the contrary. Paul describes Titus with love: he seems to have been an eager, willing helper, glad to do whatever he could to help Paul in the work of the gospel. We can only guess at the pastoral relationship he and Paul had had, that brought him to this point; another little reminder of what Paul's readers sometimes forget, the fact that those who knew Paul best couldn't do enough for him. Paul had appealed to Titus to go

93

back to Corinth almost as soon as he had come from there to meet Paul somewhere in the Macedonia region (see 7.6–7); Paul, it seems, wrote this letter soon after that meeting, and wanted Titus to hurry on ahead of him with it to Corinth so that when he himself came all would be prepared. Titus not only accepted this appeal – maybe after all he liked travelling! – but he was in any case keen to go back to Corinth where the Christians had been so eager and encouraging.

When it comes to the two 'brothers', we must assume that, as the letter is read out in Corinth, Titus will introduce them in person to the church, though that doesn't make it any the less strange that Paul doesn't name either of them here. Perhaps he is anxious that if the letter falls into the wrong hands these men might then be the targets of unwelcome attention as being possible carriers of large sums of money. In any case, the first to be introduced is well known throughout the churches because of the work of the gospel; what Paul says, literally, is 'the brother whose praise in the gospel through all the churches', leaving us to guess quite what he means (for instance, where to place the 'is' that we have to supply for the sentence to make sense). Some people have speculated that this might actually be Luke, already known throughout the churches as the author of a 'gospel' about Jesus, but since most people today think that Luke was writing at least ten or twenty years after Paul's missionary journeys this suggestion is not now as popular as once it was. The words Paul uses could equally well refer to someone who was well known as a preacher or teacher, or indeed skilled at practical matters of administration such as would be necessary if the collection was to be organized efficiently and honourably.

The other brother, referred to in verse 22, is not so well known as the first unnamed one, but Paul has seen good evidence of his sustained keenness for God's work. He refers to them both in a striking phrase in verse 23: they are messengers (literally, '**apostles**', though this word wasn't such a technical term as it later became) of the churches, and they are the **Messiah**'s glory! The idea that Jesus, not least at his final appearing, will gain glory from the fact of his followers is one Paul suggests elsewhere (e.g. 2 Thessalonians 1.10). To look at another Christian and think 'This is someone who will be part of the Messiah's glory when he appears again' is to learn to value one's fellow believers, not only as human beings made in God's image, but even more as part of the glory that will light up the whole world.

The central point of this passage, though, comes in verses 20 and 21. It isn't just that Paul is anxious for his own reputation – though, like many evangelists, he was surely aware that if anyone could ever say that he was simply doing it all to make money, that could be the kiss of death for his vocation and ministry. It is, rather, that he is desperately concerned that the world will look at the young and small Christian movement and see it, not as a variation on a well-known theme (people travelling around teaching odd doctrines as a way of earning a living), but as the radical and challenging new thing it really is. The gospel isn't about self-seeking, but self-giving. To leave any other impression is not only to sully one's own reputation, but to deny the very basis of the gospel itself. The **son of man** didn't come to be served (still less, to make money!), but to serve, and to give his life as a ransom for many (Mark 10.45). The vital work of collecting money for the benefit of the poor must not leave any impression that those who were called to this work were using it to make themselves rich.

2 CORINTHIANS 9.1–5

Please Have the Gift Ready!

¹When it comes to the service you are doing for God's people, you see, I don't need to write to you. ²For I know your eagerness,

and indeed I boasted about it to the Macedonians, saying that Achaea had been ready since last year. Your enthusiasm has stimulated most of them into action. [3]I have sent the brothers so that our boasting about you in this respect may turn out to be true – so that you may be ready, just as I said you were. [4]Otherwise, imagine what it would be like if people from Macedonia came with me and found you weren't ready! That would bring shame on us in this business, not to say on you. [5]So I thought it necessary to exhort the brothers that they should go on to you in advance, and get everything about your gracious gift in order ahead of time. You've already promised it, after all. Then it really will appear as a gift of grace, not something that has had to be extorted from you.

I knew there was something wrong the moment I walked into the shop. I used to go in two or three times every week, and knew the regular assistants quite well. But this morning the one I saw behind the counter looked as though she was, to say the least, not best pleased with life.

'So how are things, then?' I asked.

Many people would have said, 'Oh, fine', and passed it off. I would have gone away assuming that she had been bothered by something trivial, not worth talking about to a customer. But I got more than I bargained for.

She looked quickly over her shoulder, leant towards me, and spoke in a semi-whisper.

'Well, how would you like it,' she said, 'if your job had just been totally changed without anyone telling you? If you came in one day and discovered you had to work different hours? And use new *machinery*' (she spat the word out contemptuously, jerking her head towards a new computer that was sitting beside the till), 'without any training or even advice?'

'My goodness,' I said, realizing I was being enlisted as an ally in what sounded like a civil war within the small business. 'Sounds very upsetting. I'm sorry to hear about it.'

'What I don't understand', she continued, 'is why *nobody thought it all through*. That's all it would have taken: a bit of forethought and planning. Then we could all have been told, we could all have had our say, and we'd all have known where we were. But just springing it on us like this! It makes me so mad.'

I made some more sympathetic noises, paid my bill, and left, hoping the storm would soon blow over. But as I walked down the street I thought to myself: how often in the church do people rush ahead and do things without thinking them through? How often do people assume that, because they are convinced about what God wants for their church, their Sunday school, their Bible study group, their aid organization, or whatever it is, they can simply blast ahead with the plan without thinking through how each stage of the process will work, what impression people will be given, and particularly how all the people involved will *feel* about each part of the plan?

What we have in this passage is the sign that Paul cared deeply about every stage of his own planning, and thought hard about all the people involved and how they would be affected. The Corinthians might well say that he hadn't thought so hard before his previous visit. It's difficult to tell, without more information, whether Paul would have agreed with them. But this time he is determined to get it right, even if it means Titus and others making extra journeys. Every step of the process is explained and spelled out, so that everyone knows exactly where they are, and nobody can say they've had any unpleasant surprises sprung on them.

In particular, he is anxious to create a situation where three things can happen. First, he wants to be sure that when he arrives the whole collection will be ready. He doesn't want to have to begin the visit – when so many other things are riding on the mood of his arrival, as the rest of the letter makes clear – by urging them to sort out the money. He wants it all sorted out well in advance, so that, when he comes, he and they may greet one another as beloved partners in the **gospel**, without him having both to urge them to complete the collection and also, at least by implication, rebuke them for not having done so already. He does not want this to be in any way, shape or form a 'Why-haven't-you-done-this?' sort of visit.

Second, he wants their giving of money to be entirely voluntary, and for there to be no sense of them having it twisted or extorted out of them. Of course, when anybody asks a friend for money, they create a situation of pressure where a refusal may call the whole relationship into question; but Paul has been careful to remind them that they have already shown themselves eager for this project, so that he isn't asking them to do something new, but simply to complete what they had themselves already said they wanted to do. And, just to make it clear that this is the case, he wants them to finish the job before he arrives, so that there will be no suggestion or implication that they have only raised the money because he stood there and looked them meaningfully in the eye.

Third, he wants to show – as he said at the end of the previous passage, in 8.24 – that all such transactions are to be open and public, witnessed by any and all Christians. This isn't simply a private matter that he and the Corinthians can sort out behind closed doors without anyone else knowing what's going on. It's all about being open and accountable; which means that the people coming with Paul from Macedonia already know what has been planned, and will be surprised if it doesn't happen. Paul doesn't say that he actually is bringing some Christians from Macedonia with him, though it's unlikely that he would have written verse 4 if he wasn't. But he just wants to hint at the embarrassment, and even shame, that would come on him, and on them, if, having told the Macedonians (who had themselves been extremely generous, as we saw earlier) that the Corinthians were going to give generously as well, he were then to be proved wrong.

Paul has thus thought through the whole process, and wants the Corinthians both to understand the workings of his mind, and the reasons for the rather complex travel plans he has in mind for himself and his companions, and also to think through in their own right the consequences of the different courses of action that are open to them. They could, of course, sulk and refuse to co-operate; but that would bring shame on them, and on Paul, and he's just established through Titus's visit that they are eager to be fully reconciled with him. They could wait until he arrives and then co-operate; but that would make it look as though they hadn't really wanted to and were waiting for the pressure of his presence. Or they could, freely and gladly, do what they have already agreed to do, and do it before he gets there. They have a choice, but thinking it through will lead them to make the right one.

As far as we know (from Romans 15.26) they did what Paul was suggesting. If only all God's people would think things right through in our own day, and act accordingly, we too might get somewhere.

2 CORINTHIANS 9.6–15

God Loves a Cheerful Giver

[6]This is what I mean: someone who sows sparingly will reap sparingly as well. Someone who sows generously will reap generously. [7]Everyone should do as they have determined in their heart, not in a gloomy spirit or simply because they have to, since 'God loves a cheerful giver'. [8]And God is well able to lavish all his grace upon you, so that in every matter and in every way you will have enough of everything, and may be lavish in all your own good works, [9]just as the Bible says:

> They scattered their seed, they gave to the poor,
> Their righteousness endures for ever.
>
> [10]The one who supplies 'seed to be sown and bread to eat'
> will supply and increase your seed, and multiply the yield of
> your righteousness. [11]You will be enriched in every way in all
> single-hearted goodness, which is working through us to
> produce thanksgiving to God. [12]The service of this ministry
> will not only supply what God's people so badly need, but it
> will also overflow with many thanksgivings to God. [13]Through
> meeting the test of this service you will glorify God in two
> ways: first, because your confession of faith in the Messiah's
> gospel has brought you into proper order, and second, because
> you have entered into genuine and sincere partnership with
> them and with everyone. [14]What's more, they will then pray
> for you and long for you because of the surpassing grace God
> has given to you. [15]Thanks be to God for his gift, the gift we
> can never fully describe!

Imagine trying to pack an umbrella into a cardboard tube. If
you try putting the handle in first it will be difficult. Even if
the handle is straight, you will find that the metal tips of the
umbrella's struts get caught on the edge of the tube as you
struggle to push it in. You may eventually succeed, but you may
tear the umbrella, or perhaps the cardboard, in the attempt.
The answer, of course, is to turn the umbrella round so that
the pointed end goes in first. Then, even if the umbrella isn't
folded up properly, you will find that it goes in easily enough.

Something similar happens when people try to persuade
others into a course of action which they may find difficult or
challenging. Going on telling people to do something they
don't particularly want to do is like pushing an umbrella into
a tube the wrong way round. You may succeed; if you're a
forceful enough character, people may eventually do what
you want; but they won't enjoy it, and you may damage some
relationships on the way. The trick is so to turn people's minds

and imaginations around so that what had seemed forced, awkward and unnatural now seems the most natural thing of all.

Paul rounds off his careful and cautious appeal about the collection by standing back from the details of travel plans and other arrangements and outlining the world-view within which generous giving of the sort he has in mind no longer seems awkward or peculiar. It would be easy to read this passage as simply a list of wise maxims, shrewd and pithy sayings about human generosity and God's abundant goodness; but, although the passage does have that flavour, there is more to it than that. It may be just a sketch, but it's a sketch of nothing less than the whole picture of what it means to be God's people. Give people a few slogans, and you may end up simply trying to force them to do things they don't want to. Turn their minds around so that they see everything – God, the world, the church, themselves – in a different light, and the behaviour may come naturally.

As always, Paul's vision of God's people is firmly rooted in the Bible. And whenever Paul quotes a passage of the Bible, even four or five words, it's worth looking at the original passage, often the entire chapter or paragraph from which the quotation is taken, and seeing what its overall sense is. Here we have three passages, each one of which contributes more than meets the eye to what he is saying, and which together help him to construct a larger picture of who God's people are, what their goal in life should be, and how generosity in giving plays a vital part in it all.

The first passage he quotes is from a verse in Proverbs which occurs in the Greek translation of Proverbs 22.8: 'God blesses a cheerful giver.' Paul and his churches would have normally read the Bible in Greek, and the passage he quotes would have been part of that Bible, even though (for reasons that are now difficult to fathom) it isn't in the Hebrew texts, and in consequence isn't in the English and other translations we know today. But what's more important is that much of Proverbs chapter 22 as a whole is about riches and poverty, which has of course been Paul's subject now for two chapters of this letter. 'A good name', the chapter begins, 'is to be chosen instead of great riches, and grace is better than silver and gold.' Paul has been talking about 'grace' a good deal in these chapters, and the 'grace' in question often consists precisely in living for the good name of being God's people rather than hanging on to silver and gold for dear life. Several subsequent verses give instruction about riches, and verse 8 speaks of people who 'sow' wickedness and 'reap' evil, while verse 9 speaks of those who take pity on the poor being themselves supplied with food. Paul is, once more, calling to mind an entire passage, not just a single saying, since he starts this passage by talking about people 'sowing' in a meagre way or a generous way; and the word he uses for 'generously' is the same word that Proverbs uses ('blesses') for what God will do to a cheerful giver. Proverbs gives a reasonably complete portrait of a wise and God-fearing person who knows how to be generous with money. Paul wants the Corinthians to see this as a portrait of themselves.

The second passage he quotes from is Psalm 112.9, speaking again of the person who scatters blessing to the poor. Such a person, says the Psalm, has a 'righteousness' which lasts for ever. This word 'righteousness' is a puzzle to many today, since it makes people think of that unpleasant quality, 'self-righteousness'. But it's hard to know what other word to use. In the Psalms and elsewhere in the Old Testament, it regularly refers on the one hand to God's own faithfulness to the promises he made to his people, and on the other to the behaviour by which God's people demonstrate their gratitude to God for this faithfulness. In the case of the present Psalm, the whole poem is a celebration of those who fear and trust the Lord, and in particular of their generosity and merciful behaviour towards their neighbours, particularly the poor. Once again, Paul is inviting the Corinthians to step inside the biblical portrait and discover a whole new identity, not simply to do something strange because he tells them to.

But the real climax comes in the third passage. God, says Paul, provides 'seed for the sower and bread to eat', quoting Isaiah 55.10. Isaiah 55 is the glorious invitation to all and sundry to come and feast on God's rich bounty, because God is making a new creation in which everything will be renewed. This new creation, achieved through the death and **resurrection** of the Servant of the Lord in Isaiah 53, is based on the **covenant** renewal celebrated in Isaiah 54, and will come about because God will 'sow' his **Word** in the same way that he sends rain and snow to provide seed-corn and bread. This picture is exactly the same as the large-scale picture Paul has been drawing throughout the letter: God's new creation (5.17), based on God's new covenant (chapter 3), accomplished through the death and resurrection of Jesus the **Messiah**, and now at work in the world through the preaching of the **gospel**.

What Paul is urging them to do is to think of themselves, as it were, this way round, and to discover that, if they realize they are characters in the great drama which is going forwards, then the generosity he is urging will come naturally. In the normal and healthy Christian life, everything proceeds from God's generosity, and everything returns to God in thanksgiving (verse 12; compare 1.11 and 4.15). Grace, generosity and gratitude: these are not optional extras of Christian living, but are the very heart of it all.

2 CORINTHIANS 10.1–11

The Battle for the Mind

[1]Think of the Messiah, meek and gentle; then think of me, Paul – yes, Paul himself! – making his appeal to you. You

know what I'm like: I'm humble when I'm face to face with you, but I'm bold when I'm away from you! [2]Please, please don't put me in the position of having to be bold when I'm with you, of having to show how confident I dare to be when I'm standing up to people who think we are behaving in a merely human way. [3]Yes, we are mere humans, but we don't fight the war in a merely human way. [4]The weapons we use for the fight, you see, are not merely human; they carry a power from God that can tear down fortresses! We tear down clever arguments, [5]and every proud notion that sets itself up against the knowledge of God. We take every thought prisoner and make it obey the Messiah. [6]We are holding ourselves in readiness to punish every disobedience, when your obedience is complete.

[7]Look at what's in front of your face. If anyone trusts that they belong to the Messiah, let them calculate it once more: just as they belong to the Messiah, so also do we! [8]For if I do indeed boast a bit too enthusiastically about the authority which the Lord has given me – which is for building you up, not for pulling you down! – I shan't be ashamed. [9]I wouldn't want to look as if I were trying to frighten you with my letters. [10]I know what they say: 'His letters are serious and powerful, but when he arrives in person he is weak, and his words aren't worth bothering about.' [11]Anyone like that should reckon on this: the way we talk in letters, when we're absent, will be how we behave when we're present.

It was pitch dark, and the prickles from the bush I was hiding behind were sticking through my clothes and into my skin. I couldn't see anything, but I could hear, very faintly, someone coming along the path. All chance of reaching my own goal had disappeared; the only question was whether I would get caught. The prickles got worse, and despite my best attempts to stay still I just had to move, ever so slightly. He heard me and was on to me like a flash. Within a few moments I had had to put on a different armband and join the other side.

It was a game, of course – a wonderful night-time adventure at a boys' camp in the Scottish highlands. There were two teams, sometimes more, each trying to capture the others' flag, hidden some distance from each other across a stretch of wild hillside. And one of the ways the battle progressed was that certain members of each team were given a special role: to capture members of the opposition and force them to change sides. Gradually one side would become dominant and be able to overpower the opposition.

In verses 3, 4 and 5 Paul describes his strategy in the battle for the mind. At its heart is the principle he states in verse 5: we take every thought prisoner, and make it obey the **Messiah**. It is a bold intention, and this whole passage is about boldness, the boldness of the **apostle** who somehow balances the meekness and gentleness of the Messiah with the boldness that tears down strongholds. The death and **resurrection** of King Jesus are here, as always, central to Paul's understanding of everything. Now, as he turns back to the theme which dominated the early part of the letter – his standing with the Corinthians, and the attacks that some in the church have made against his style, his ministry, his very apostleship – he shows what lies at the heart of the boldness he is capable of using not only when far away and writing letters but also when he's personally present. He doesn't want to have to use that boldness, but he will if necessary. And they need to know where it comes from.

It comes from Paul's thought-out and long-practised strategy for the war he's engaged in. Elsewhere (e.g. Romans 13.12, Ephesians 6.10–20, and 1 Thessalonians 5.8) he describes the weapons he uses for the fight; here he says what they're used *for*. They are what you need for the battle against all ideas, arguments, philosophies and world-views that set themselves up against the knowledge of the true God. Paul knew what he was talking about: the world of ancient Greece,

Turkey, Syria and Palestine was teeming with religions and cults, philosophies and teachings, dark magic and high-flown wisdom, arcane rituals and passionately held ideals. But there was only one place where the power of the true God, the creator of the world, had been fully and finally unveiled; and that was in the death and resurrection of Jesus, the Messiah. Paul was not content to offer people a new religious experience, another option to be added to the rich pluralism his world already knew. He was determined to confront the human-made systems of thought which, though usually containing some glimmers of truth, actually led people away from knowledge of the true God rather than towards him.

For this, of course, Paul was cordially hated by many in the ancient world, just as he is resented by people in our own day who prefer an easy-going pluralism to the idea that there really is one God and that he really has made himself known uniquely and decisively in Jesus the Messiah, the world's true Lord. So Paul found himself facing a battle on two fronts; not only to win the argument against rival views, but to make it clear that such a confrontation was appropriate in the first place.

The trouble with confrontations over ideas, though, is that it's easy to make the mistake of thinking that every position, every philosophy, which isn't explicitly Christian must be totally and utterly wrong. Paul knew better. He was not a dualist. All truth is God's truth. All truth can be twisted to serve the ends of human pride and arrogance, and that happens far too frequently. But it can be straightened out again; and the way to do that is to 'take it captive', to make it change armbands, to bring it on to the right side. There is no insight, no vision of truth, so noble and lofty that it cannot be perverted and made an instrument of human pride. Likewise, there is no small glimmer of light, no faint echo of reality, so small or corrupt that it cannot be taken into the service of the world's creator and rightful Lord.

That word itself, 'Lord', is a good example. In Paul's day, Caesar was Lord of the world, and saviour as well. Paul took these grand titles and gave them to Jesus, snatching the enemy's proud boast from under his nose. He did the same with many other ideas, such as the 'fullness of divinity' in Colossians 2.9, where he picks up a phrase in use in some of the religions of the time and declares that what it really refers to is found in Jesus. Perhaps the best-known example of this is the altar, in Athens, to the Unknown God. According to Acts 17.23, Paul used that as his starting point to talk about the one true God who could now be truly known in Jesus, the Messiah and Lord.

The battle for the mind remains central to the church's task, in this and every age. But it doesn't just have to be fought by Christians against those outside the church. It has to be fought inside the church as well, and that's what Paul is beginning once more to do in this section of the letter. He now knows that the church as a whole is well disposed towards him (7.5–16). But there are still some teachers who might be inclined to rebel, to say about him what they'd always said: that he wasn't half as good a speaker as he was a writer, and that, though he sounded imposing when far away, he was actually insignificant in person. He was, in any case, just another human being doing what all human beings do, not a truly 'spiritual' person as some of them claimed to be.

The point of this present passage is to say: if that's the challenge, I'm ready to take it on. My whole ministry, after all, is all about opposing proud arguments that set themselves up against the true knowledge of God. If that's my speciality in my teaching towards outsiders, do you suppose I won't do the same if I'm confronted by people in the church itself?

Many people today find that this strikes a worrying note. They don't like thinking of a Christian teacher being so confrontative. But we can't have it both ways. Paul has been accused of being weak and insignificant, of stringing together ideas as best he can. He is going to show that they are mistaken; but just watch how he does it. He is going to boast, but it will be an upside-down sort of boast. The argument he will now mount will itself be a fine example of the principle he has stated. The ideas of boasting and boldness will themselves be taken captive and made to serve and obey the **gospel** of the Messiah.

2 CORINTHIANS 10.12–18

Boasting in the Lord

[12]We wouldn't dare, you see, to figure out where we belong on some scale or other, or compare ourselves with people who commend themselves. They measure themselves by one another, and compare themselves with one another. That just shows how silly they are! [13]But when we boast, we don't do so without having something to measure ourselves by; we boast according to the measure of the rule God has given us to measure ourselves by, and that rule includes our work with you! [14]We weren't going beyond our assigned limits when we reached you; we were the first to get as far as you with the gospel of the Messiah. [15]We don't boast without a measuring rule in the work someone else has done. This is what we hope for: that, as your faith increases, we will be given a much larger space for work, according to our rule, [16]which is to announce the gospel in the lands beyond you, not to boast in what has already been accomplished through the rule someone else has been given. [17]'Anyone who boasts should boast in the Lord!' [18]Who is it, after all, who gains approval? It isn't the person who commends himself. It's the person whom the Lord commends.

I took my son to school on a snowy morning. He was wearing boots, gloves, a woolly hat and a thick coat. When we got there – he was about five years old – we had quite a struggle to take it all off and get him ready for classes. To help with the boots, I sat down on the bench in the changing room; it was made for little children, and was only a foot or so high. As I sat there, almost on the floor itself, another little boy came in. He paused a moment, looked me up and down (my head was about level with his) and then declared, 'My Daddy's bigger than you.'

It's not exactly the same point as the one Paul is making, but it's not far off. It's easy to leap to conclusions when you're sizing people up, and you need to pause for a moment and ask yourself if you're using the right scale, if you're comparing like with like, if you've taken all the relevant facts into consideration. And the trouble with the people Paul is now talking about is that they've reached a snap judgment, based on a faulty way of measuring themselves and other people.

What is at stake here is the same problem we met earlier in the letter: the question of people who are 'recommending themselves', and who are even suggesting that if Paul wants to come back to Corinth he ought to get himself 'letters of recommendation' – as though you might need official permission to go into the house you built yourself, where your own family live! Just as we don't know who it was that Paul was sending along with Titus at the end of chapter 8, so we don't know who exactly these people are who are 'commending themselves' (verses 12 and 18). As he says a little more about them in the next chapter, we get the sense that they are either **apostles**, or perhaps messengers from the apostles: Jewish Christians, who are trying to pull the Corinthian church away from their loyalty to Paul. But these people don't seem to be like the Jewish Christians Paul had to battle with in Galatia, who were urging the new converts to get **circumcised**. If that had been their aim, Paul would certainly have argued against it, and we would have known all about it. Instead, they seem to be wanting merely to have the Corinthian church hold them in high esteem, to be regarded as great teachers and leaders. To that end, they have been trying to make out that Paul is insignificant and not worth bothering about.

But what standard are they using? That's the question Paul insists on asking. They appear simply to be comparing themselves with themselves; if three small people stand side by side, they can convince themselves that they are all really quite tall – until a really tall person comes into the room. Or, again, I might imagine to myself that I am really seven feet tall; but if there's a rule on the wall that I can measure myself by, an objective standard, marked out in feet and inches (or metres and centimetres), I will soon learn my mistake. When Paul thinks about the work he's done, the tasks he's been carrying out, he isn't simply looking at other people for comparison. He is looking at the actual measure God has set up, the rule on the wall which consists of the commission God gave him in the first place. He isn't going to compare himself with anyone else. The only comparison that matters is whether he matches up to the standard God set for him.

And that standard, that rule, that commission, includes – the Corinthian church itself! This shows how ridiculous it is for them to suppose that new teachers can come in and try to take over. Founding the church in Corinth was part of the job God gave Paul to do. He did it; he belongs to them and they to him, in the intimate family relationship of the **Messiah**'s people. That is the point that he must make clear before he can go any further. If there's any measuring to be done, any assessment of who's who in the story of the Corinthian church, you simply can't take it away from Paul: he was the one who went there and announced the **good news** of the Messiah. Whatever else has happened since, that's what he did; it was within his commission that he should do so; and (he implies) the fact that there's a church there to this day is testimony to the fact that the Lord has commended him for doing it.

And that's not all. He's now hoping to develop the work still further. As we saw in the very first verse of the letter, the **gospel** has spread outside Corinth to other parts of southern Greece. Paul is now hoping that it will do so more and more. What this will take on the Corinthians' part, he says in verse 15, is more *faith*: not faith in a different God, but faith that the God they have already believed in will do new and bigger things than they have yet imagined. If only they would stop fussing about styles of leadership, personality cults and the like, and get back to the real task of the gospel, this could easily come about.

In all this Paul may perhaps have a specific problem in view, which he just hints at in verses 15 and 16, and comes back to in Romans 15.20. The specific commission he has received from the Lord is to be a pioneer missionary and evangelist; that is, to announce the good news in places where it has never been heard before. That is the 'rule' by which he should be measured. He doesn't mind what other commissions the Lord has given to other people, as long as he is faithful to his own. He may perhaps have in mind the famous agreement he made with Peter and the other Jerusalem apostles in Galatians 2.9, that they should go to Jewish communities and he should go to **Gentile** ones, though no doubt this was harder to implement in practice (since Jews lived all over the Mediterranean world, in among Gentiles) than it sounded at the time. What he is most concerned about, though, is that he shouldn't be thought to be poaching on someone else's patch, and that other people shouldn't claim to have the status of 'founding apostle' on territory that God had given to him.

What it all comes down to is the true nature of the Christian 'boast': anyone who boasts should boast in the Lord! He's already quoted this (it comes from Jeremiah 9.23) in the first letter to Corinth (1.31), where it stood as a sign that all the different things the church might want to boast of, not least its social and cultural advancement through teachers with more rhetoric than substance, had to be subjected to the humiliation of the cross. Now he quotes it again with a similar though slightly different aim. He wants to warn the church against those who 'commend themselves', but are not commended by the Lord; and he wants to prepare the way for one of his own most powerful pieces of writing, the 'boasting' in chapter 11 which will show them, once and for all, what it means to have one's whole life reshaped around the Messiah and his cross. Is it boasting you want? he asks. Then boasting you shall have; but don't expect it to look like what you imagined. 'In the Lord', after all, everything has been turned upside down and inside out. That's what must happen to boasting as well.

2 CORINTHIANS 11.1–6

Super-Apostles?

[1]I'd be glad if you would bear with me in a little bit of foolishness. Yes: bear with me, please! [2]I'm jealous over you, and it's God's own jealousy: I arranged to marry you off, like a pure virgin, to the one man I presented you to, namely the Messiah. [3]But the serpent tricked Eve with its cunning, and in the same way I'm afraid that your minds may be corrupted from the single-mindedness and purity which the Messiah's people should have. [4]For if someone comes and announces a different Jesus than the one we announced to you, or if you receive a different spirit, one you hadn't received before, or a different gospel, one you hadn't accepted before, you put up with that all right. [5]According to my calculations, you see, I am every bit as good as these super-apostles. [6]I may be untutored in speaking, but that certainly doesn't apply to my knowledge. Surely that's been made quite clear to you, in every way and on every point!

Many movies have as a stock theme the marriage service that

goes wrong at the last minute. The famous 1960s movie, *The Graduate*, ended up with the hero dashing into the church where his true love was about to marry someone else, and snatching her off just before it was too late. More recently the theme was worked over quite thoroughly in a film called *Runaway Bride*, where the bride wasn't snatched away by someone else but simply kept running away of her own accord. Interruptions to weddings are a stock theme in novels, too, going back at least as far as *Jane Eyre*.

Paul imagines himself as the father of the bride, arranging a marriage for his daughter. (In his world, especially his Jewish world, most marriages would be arranged by the parents, often when the bride at least was, by our standards, very young.) Everything has been agreed; the husband-to-be is delighted, and so is the bride – or at least she was; but the father is suddenly worried that she's going to get itchy feet, and run off with someone else. The bride, of course, is the church in Corinth; the bridegroom is the **Messiah** himself; here as elsewhere, Paul has taken the biblical theme of Israel as the bride of **YHWH** and has transposed it into the theme of the church as the bride of the Messiah (see, e.g., Romans 7.4; Ephesians 5.25–33). But while his back is turned, the bride starts eyeing other men instead . . .

At which point Paul draws on another well-known stock theme in Jewish and Christian thought: the temptation and rebellion in Genesis 3. (This, too, he echoes in other places, such as Romans 5.12–21 and 7.9–11.) Elsewhere he highlights Adam as the one whose sin caused all the problems. But here, because of the other illustration he's using, he refers only to Eve, and to the trickery by which the serpent beguiled her into taking the forbidden fruit. Paul seems to be worried about the danger of a second 'Fall': the 'new creation' which he spoke of in 5.17, which is after all at the heart of the whole **gospel** (see Galatians 6.15), might be followed by a 'new fall', and – though he doesn't seriously think this is going to happen – chaos might come again.

So what is the problem? It looks as though Paul is now accusing the teachers (who came to Corinth after he left) of something more serious than anything he's mentioned before. Not only are they trying to persuade the Christians that the proper style of leadership is something more showy and impressive than anything they'd seen in Paul. Not only are they highlighting practices of spirituality and worship which accentuate social divisions. They are actually offering people a different spirit, a different gospel, and ultimately a different Jesus! What can Paul mean?

Some have thought that these chapters were aimed at a different set of teachers than the ones he was opposing in the first six chapters. Maybe, some have suggested, there were after all some even newer teachers in Corinth, who were trying to persuade the church in the same sort of way that the rival teachers in Galatia had done. There, too, after all, Paul accuses them of preaching 'another gospel' (Galatians 1.6–9). But I think it's more likely that he has the same teachers in mind as he had earlier in the letter, and that he's simply homing in at last on what his real criticism of them is. It isn't that they are actually talking about a completely different person, a different 'Jesus'; there were, it's true, plenty of Jewish men with that name in the first century, but it is highly improbable that they were referring to someone other than the teacher from Nazareth who was crucified under Pontius Pilate. It isn't that they claim to be offering an entirely different spirit from the one the Corinthians received; there were many 'spirits' on offer in the religious world of the day, but the teachers were presumably claiming to be inspired by the same **spirit** that had been at work in the church all along. It isn't that they are announcing a gospel which has nothing in common with the one Paul summarizes in 1 Corinthians 15.3–8. No: the problem is more subtle than that.

The problem is that they are talking glibly about Jesus; they are claiming the power of the spirit; they are enthusiastic about the gospel – but there is a subtle and all-important difference between their Jesus, their spirit, their gospel, and the true one. The true Jesus was the one who suffered unspeakably. The true spirit is the one who groans within the suffering of the world (Romans 8.18–27). The true gospel is the message of the crucified Lord. And the teachers who have come to Corinth after Paul left have been quietly toning down this hard, rough edge of the gospel. It doesn't fit with their social and cultural aspirations. It doesn't sound so good in terms of rhetorical style. In particular, it doesn't give them the reputation and status they are hoping for. If you really believe in the suffering Messiah, and pattern your life accordingly, they think, you might end up looking like . . . yes. Like Paul. And that's what they don't want.

By this stage of the letter, Paul is actually quite confident that the bride is not going to run off with someone else. The news which Titus has brought from Corinth (7.5–16) has been good. The church as a whole is firmly on Paul's side, and is longing to see him again and to be reconciled fully. But the teachers haven't gone away. They might now suppose that they could wait for Paul to arrive, and then show him up again as a fool, an ignoramus, as someone lacking in basic social and cultural skills. And that sort of confrontation, with all its potential for confusion among ordinary church members, is the last thing Paul wants when he arrives. So he must deal with the problem before it happens. Is the bride going to run off after someone else who winks at her through the window? Or is she going to stay where she is and be faithful to the Messiah, the suffering Messiah, the crucified and risen Messiah, the Messiah whose dying and rising is being lived out in Paul's own ministry?

2 CORINTHIANS 11.7–15

No, They Are False Apostles!

[7]Did I then commit a sin when I humbled myself in order to exalt you? When I announced the gospel of God to you without charging you for it? [8]I robbed other churches by accepting payment from them in order to serve you; [9]and when I was with you, and was in need of anything, I didn't lay a burden on anybody, because my needs were more than met by the brothers who came from Macedonia. That's how I stopped myself from being a burden to you – and I intend to carry on in the same way. [10]As the Messiah's truthfulness is in me, this boast of mine will not be silenced in the regions of Achaea. [11]Why? Because I don't love you? God knows . . . !

[12]I'm going to continue to do what I've always done, so as to cut off any opportunity (for those who want such an opportunity!) for anyone to find something to boast of in the same way that we do. [13]Such people are false apostles! The only work they do is to deceive! They transform themselves so that they look like apostles of the Messiah – [14]and no wonder. The satan himself transforms himself to look like an angel of light, [15]so it isn't surprising if his servants transform themselves to look like servants of righteousness. They will end up where their deeds are taking them.

The door to my study was open when the telephone rang in the hall, so I couldn't help overhearing the conversation, or rather this end of it. And what I heard was quite disturbing.

'How could you think I imagined that . . . ?'

'But I didn't say anything of the kind . . .'

'No, you've got it wrong; I don't know who told you that story . . .'

'Look, I'm very sorry, but I honestly think you've misjudged the whole situation . . .'

'But I never have thought that, and I never would!'

Eventually calm was restored, but I was left still wondering what on earth the problem had been. Curiosity, of course, overcame me, and I came out of the study, admitted I'd heard all the protestations of innocence, and then received the whole explanation.

The explanation, of course, is what we can't have with Paul's letters, though we always wish we could. (Unless some archaeologist digs up some more ancient documents, and they turn out to contain some more letters of either Paul or his opponents . . . now that *would* be exciting.) And, of all Paul's writings, this passage is one of the most tantalizing. We are left to fill in the gaps, to work out, if we can, what on earth had been said by these teachers in Corinth that had left the church with so many misunderstandings about Paul's work, his motives, his feelings, his plans and his general behaviour. Why did he have to explain himself on so many points at once?

The first point takes us back to things that were said in 1 Corinthians 9. There Paul explains (in the course of another discussion; Paul never seems content with making one point if two or three will do, all at the same time) that he had quite deliberately not taken any payment, even his basic living and travelling expenses, from the church in Corinth. Other **apostles** did so, and Paul strongly defends the principle that they should; but he has chosen not to, in order to make the **gospel** free of charge (1 Corinthians 9.18, picked up by verse 7 of the present passage). This has always been his 'boast'. He seems to have been very concerned that nobody in Achaea should ever be able to accuse him of preaching the gospel in order to get rich. Or perhaps (this is precisely the sort of point where we are reduced to guesswork) he was determined that nobody in Achaea should imagine that they owned him, that by paying

117

him for his services they would be able to control him, to make him do things their way, or to trim his message to their tastes.

But Paul now finds he's being damned if he does and damned if he doesn't. Having bent over backwards not to be a burden to them – and perhaps to make clear one of the points we've just suggested – he now finds himself accused of not really loving them, because he's allowed other Christians to help him out financially but has refused all help from Corinth! (And, of course, just to confuse matters still further, he *is* now asking them for money, but it's not for himself but for Jerusalem.) To be fair, it must have been puzzling for the Corinthian Christians to have people coming from Macedonia to keep Paul in funds. But he had his reasons for organizing things that way, and had explained it to them carefully.

Anyway, this questioning of his motives and practice was clearly coming from one particular source, or one particular group of people: the 'super-apostles', as he calls them with heavy irony in verse 5. Now he drops the irony and declares, forcefully, that they aren't 'super-apostles' at all; they are *false* apostles, proclaiming and teaching a false gospel. Worse: they are servants of the **satan**. That is one of the strongest accusations anyone can make, but it's not simply a bit of miscellaneous religious name-calling. The teachers in Corinth had been *accusing* Paul of all kinds of things of which he knew he wasn't guilty. In traditional biblical and Jewish thinking, the 'satan' was the accuser, the Director of Public Prosecutions for the heavenly court. It was his job to accuse people, to brings charges against all wrongdoers. In order to have charges to bring, the satan seems to have taken to whispering ideas into people's ears . . . and so became the tempter as well as the prosecutor. And if people failed to respond to the whispered suggestions, the satan was quite capable of making false accusations instead.

That is precisely what Paul sees going on in Corinth. The teachers have been trying to convince the church of all sorts of accusations against Paul, and he is determined to show that they are false; but what does that say about those who have been bringing the charges? That they are in the service of the **accuser**. This is of course dangerous language, and Paul is well aware of what he is doing. He doesn't say these things lightly, and has waited until now, having worked through most of the main issues he wants to address, to build up to his final appeal. And he finds he needs to shock his hearers into realizing that they must choose: if the teachers are right, Paul is wrong, but if Paul is right – as most people in the church apparently now believe – the teachers are not merely offering a harmless local variation of the gospel. They are undoing its work, by failing to follow through on the deepest meanings of the cross and **resurrection**. They are, whether they know it or not, and whether they look like it or not, acting in the service of the enemy.

The history of the church shows, alas, that often when people in the church have been doing truly diabolical things (genocide, for instance, or child-abuse), the church has failed to name these as what they are; and that, often enough, people have been only too ready to accuse one another of being in league with the satan when what was going on was a political power-game. The generous-hearted liberal who hates to say anyone at all is wrong can easily fail to spot real evil. The narrow-minded conservative who hates to say anyone else is right can easily label good as evil. We should not mistake Paul for one of the latter. He was involved in a battle for the gospel: would the message of Jesus be turned into a local variation on the prevailing philosophical and religious culture, or would it remain the agent of God's new creation?

2 CORINTHIANS 11.16–21a

The Boasting of a Reluctant Fool

[16]I'll say it again: don't let anyone think I'm a fool! But if they do – well, all right then, welcome me as a fool, so that I can do a little bit of boasting! [17]What I'm going to say now, I'm not saying as if it came from the Lord, but as if I was a fool, as if I really did want to indulge myself in this kind of boasting. [18]Plenty of people are boasting in human terms, after all, so why shouldn't I boast as well? [19]After all, you put up with fools readily enough, since you are so wise yourselves. [20]You put up with it if someone makes you their slave, or if they eat up your property, or overpower you, or give themselves airs, or slap you in the face. [21]Well, I'm ashamed to say it: we weren't strong enough for that!

There was a party going on downstairs, but the company president wasn't at it. Normally he enjoyed a good party with the best of them, but today wasn't the day. He knew the business was heading for difficult times, and there was a great deal of hard work to be done if they were to stay afloat in an uncertain economic future. They had a fine product, they had done well in the past, but the world was changing and if they didn't keep ahead of the game they would be finished. There wouldn't be any reason for a party then.

The noise of laughter and singing drifted up to his office and irritated him. They didn't understand how serious the situation was. And he suspected he knew who was leading the fun and games: a couple of middle-ranking executives who never quite did a proper day's work, who were always ready to show off to the others, always the life and soul of the party, but who were somehow always absent when the really difficult tasks had to be faced. He sighed, and turned back to the papers on his desk.

As he did so, there was a tap on the door. It was his assistant.

'Sorry to trouble you, sir,' he said. 'I know this is a bad time and you've got better things to do. But a couple of us were just thinking it might really help if you could come and join the party, even if it's only for five minutes or so. People would like to see you.'

The laughter and merry noises came, more loudly, through the open door. He'd never be able to concentrate now anyway. He got up from the desk, loosened his tie, and with a wry smile to the assistant he came downstairs.

A huge cheer went up as they all saw him. And there, just as he'd guessed, were the two executives. They were organizing a complicated but silly game involving a tub of water, paper hats, apples and pears, and a coin. The point seemed to be to make people look as ridiculous as possible while trying to eat an apple, or, for the bold ones, to pick the coin off the bottom of the tub with their teeth. Several people had been trying it without much success, and there was much splashing, giggling and cheering.

The president accepted a drink, and stood watching from the edge of the crowd, thinking of the papers on his desk and the future of the company. But then one of the ringleaders said in a loud voice,

'I know who'd be good at this! Our president! Just the man for a good apple!'

The happy throng cheered and looked across at him. His assistant shot him an anxious glance. It was clear they were simply wanting to make him look stupid, to have a laugh at his expense. For a moment he hesitated, then, to more cheers, he took off his tie and stepped forwards. There was a glint in his eye. He remembered playing this game twenty, no, thirty years ago, as a teenager. There was a technique. He might just be able to . . .

They put a paper hat on his head, and tied his hands behind his back. He knelt down on the floor in front of the tub.

Suddenly the room went quiet. Then, in a flash, he plunged his head through the bobbing apples and pears, straight down to the bottom. A second later he brought it up again and, in a single movement, stood up with the coin between his teeth.

The biggest cheer of the day rang around the room. He pulled a hand free and held up the coin, motioning for silence.

'All right,' he said. 'You've seen I can play the fool. But let me tell you this. I know how to find money, even at the bottom of a bucket of water, and you lads obviously don't. If you want to find coins in your pockets, you'd better watch what I do over the next week or two. Otherwise you're going to drown at the bottom of the tub. After all,' (here he looked straight at the two ringleaders) 'you're prepared to put up with people telling you to do silly things. How about putting up with me telling you how to make this company a roaring success?'

And with that he finished his drink, put on his tie, shook hands with the ringleaders, and went back upstairs to his desk.

Paul was not a company director, and he wasn't interested in making money, but in other respects this is the position he was in. He could see that the church in Corinth had allowed itself to be taken off to a party – a party of exciting rhetoric, a new style of teaching, a chance to become famous or at least to enjoy being close to other people who seemed to be celebrities. It was quite a dramatic change from the humdrum and often difficult lives many of them led. Fancy being with people who were so clever, so witty, such good speakers, such profound thinkers, had had such wonderful experiences, were such a success! And as the party progressed these people did of course make demands – they bossed others around, they insisted on being paid a lot of money, they were sometimes even rude or dismissive to Christians who couldn't understand what they were saying . . . but, after all, they were celebrated, important, leading figures, so you had to put up with it or you'd look a fool . . .

And Paul has decided that he's going to play the fool himself. They have forced him into it. He's going to come and join the party; but there's a glint in his eye which says they're going to get more than they have bargained for. He knows who the ringleaders are, what they've been up to, and how, if their type of Christianity were to catch on, the **gospel** wouldn't be doing its proper work in Corinth, Achaea or anywhere else. They have been bossing people around, and the people have put up with it. Very well, let them now put up with him playing the fool for a few moments. They have been boasting of all kinds of things; all right, he's going to boast, too, and we'll see who wins the game.

He is quite clear that what he is about to say is not serious gospel teaching. He doesn't want anyone to imagine he would go through all this, left to his own devices. But at the same time we begin to see, and the next two passages will confirm this, that the gospel is shining through even what he calls foolishness. He has decided to boast, not of the sort of things the rival teachers have been boasting about, but about a different sort of thing entirely. He has already spoken of his life as an **apostle**, and of the many ways in which he has shared the sufferings of the **Messiah**, confident of the glory that is yet to be revealed (see 4.7–12 and 6.3–10 and, behind those again, 1 Corinthians 4.6–13). Now he is going to crown those passages with yet another, full of irony: he is teasing them, taking them at their word but making his own point, joining in the foolish fun but knowing a trick or two that will take them by surprise and enable him to make his own point. Is it boasting you want? Boasting you shall have. Is it rhetoric you want? Rhetoric you shall have. At the start of the earlier letter he had spoken of the foolishness of God which was wiser than humans, and the weakness of God which was stronger than humans (1 Corinthians 1.25). Now, in a spectacular burst of 'foolishness', he is going to boast of his weakness, thereby showing what it means to be truly wise, and truly strong.

Simply at the level of strategy and tactics, this is a bold move, and I wonder how many church leaders would dare attempt the equivalent in their own settings. At the level of content, it is bolder still. Paul is staking everything on his belief that the gospel of the crucified and risen Jesus is indeed true, and that by letting it have its effect in every area of life it will carry its own power.

2 CORINTHIANS 11.21b–33

Boasting of Weaknesses

21bWhatever anyone else dares to boast about (I'm talking nonsense, remember), I'll boast as well. 22Are they Hebrews? So am I. Are they Israelites? So am I. Are they the seed of Abraham? So am I. 23Are they servants of the Messiah? – I'm talking like a raving madman – I'm a better one. I've worked harder, been in prison more often, been beaten more times than I can count, and I've often been close to death. 24Five times I've had the Jewish beating, forty lashes less one. 25Three times I was beaten with rods; once I was stoned; three times I was shipwrecked; I was adrift in the sea for a night and a day. 26I've been constantly travelling, facing dangers from rivers, dangers from brigands, dangers from my own people, dangers from foreigners, dangers in the town, dangers in the countryside, dangers at sea, dangers from false believers. 27I've toiled and laboured, I've burnt the candle at both ends, I've been hungry and thirsty, I've often gone without food altogether, I've been cold and naked.

28Quite apart from all that, I have this daily pressure on me, my care for all the churches. 29Who is weak and I'm not weak? Who is offended without me burning with shame?

30If I must boast, I will boast of my weaknesses. 31The God and father of the Lord Jesus, who is blessed for ever, knows that I'm not lying: [32]in Damascus, King Aretas, the local ruler, was guarding the city of Damascus so that he could capture me, [33]but I was let down in a basket through a window and over the wall, and I escaped his clutches.

You can see the war memorial from the other side of the valley. It stands on the slope just below the main school buildings, a simple but elegant cloister of grey stone, containing the names of boys from the school who died in the great wars of the twentieth century. It is a sobering, serious monument.

But the place of greatest honour is the special monument to four former pupils. Each of them received the Victoria Cross: the highest military honour it's possible to attain in the British forces. Some of them received it posthumously; that has often been the case with awards of the 'VC', since many who do the bravest things, who put their own lives at risk to win a victory, or to rescue others from danger, pay the ultimate penalty.

In the world of ancient Rome, where military might and bravery was regarded as one of the highest of the virtues, the nearest equivalent to the Victoria Cross was the award known as the *corona muralis*, or 'crown of the wall'. It was a literal crown, made to look like the wall of a city, complete with gates and battlements. A marble statue of the goddess *Tyche* ('Lady Luck'), dating to the generation or so after Paul, has been found by archaeologists in Corinth, wearing one of these crowns. Clearly everyone would know what it was, and, equally important, why people were awarded it.

The *corona muralis* was awarded, and had been for many centuries by Paul's day, for one military achievement in particular. One of the central methods of ancient warfare was the siege, where the attacking army would camp around a town or city and try to force it to submit. Battering rams and other assaults on the gates might well be resisted. The town might have its own food and water supply, and could last for several months. So the crucial step would be for the attacking army to make long ladders and put them up against the walls, making a way for soldiers to get up the ladders, over the walls, and into the city.

You only have to think about that for a moment to see how dangerous it was. The defenders on the walls would try to push the ladders over backwards, preferably when there were several soldiers half way up. They would shoot arrows down at you, or pour boiling liquids on top of you. If you did make it to the top, they would be ready with all kinds of weapons to attack you and throw you back over the wall. Since only one attacker could go over the top at a time on any one ladder, you would certainly be outnumbered.

So – as an obvious incentive to this almost crazy bravery – the *corona muralis*, the 'crown of the wall', was awarded to the soldier who, during the siege, *was the first one over the wall.* Of course, very often it might be awarded posthumously: the first one over the wall might well not live to tell the tale. But, equally importantly, whoever was in fact the first one up the ladder and into the city would be the only person on his own side who would know that he *was* the first. Anybody could go home and say 'actually, I was the first one . . .' and many people wouldn't believe them. They'd think they were just boasting. So, in order to claim the 'crown of the wall', the person who actually was the first one over the wall had to return to Rome and swear a solemn oath, invoking the gods to witness that he was telling the truth. 'I swear before the holy gods, who know I'm telling the truth, that, when we were attacking the city, I was the first one over the wall.' And the crown would be awarded.

This is the only possible explanation of why Paul tells the story of his escape from Damascus in verses 32 and 33, and of why he prefaces this story with a solemn oath that the God and father of the Lord Jesus knows he isn't lying. He is listing his achievements; he is boasting; he is celebrating all his triumphs; and this one is the last and greatest of them all. Only (and this is the point of the whole passage) *he is boasting of all the wrong things.* And his escape from Damascus was the climax of the list, the equivalent of the *corona muralis.*

Corinth was a Roman colony, and like some other colonies did its best to be even more like the mother city than the mother city itself. Its Roman culture went deep. The local people were proud of it. And in Roman culture one of the standard things that every public figure could do was to list his achievements ('his', because the sort of achievements that counted were the sort that only men would do). I held this or that public office. I was quaestor in such-and-such a year, I was praetor when so-and-so was consul, I was the governor of this or that province, I gave money for some wonderful gladiatorial displays, I was elected consul (the highest office in the land when Rome was a republic, and still important under the emperors), I built a theatre, I led an army, I fought a war, I celebrated a triumph, I won a medal . . . on and on and on, I and I and I. Go to any museum with ancient inscriptions and you'll see several lists just like that, so familiar that most of it can be abbreviated into well-known formulae. And if that was how the well-known, high-profile public figures behaved, the same pattern would be worked out all down the social scale, with people who never made it to high office still eager to celebrate their own achievements in whatever sphere of life they lived in.

Throughout his two letters to Corinth, Paul has been aware that the young church is in danger of being sucked in to the ordinary cultural life of their city and district. And the teachers who have influenced the church in his absence have been going in exactly that direction. They have commended themselves, they have boasted of their achievements, they have wallowed in a culture of fame and success and showy rhetoric. Now, to answer them, Paul lists his own 'achievements', all of them things that any normal person in the Roman world would be too ashamed even to mention, let alone to celebrate. And, as the climax of the whole list, he declares with a solemn oath that when the going got really tough he was the first one over the wall – running away, being let down on a rope in a basket. He is claiming an upside-down *corona muralis*.

He is, of course, teasing them to bits. At one level he is deadly serious, but this passage is also a wonderful comic parody. Even those in Corinth who were annoyed at having their favourite hobby caricatured in this way must still have found it clever and amusing. Paul is at last writing his own 'letter of recommendation', but he's like someone applying for a job by listing all the things that would normally disqualify him straight away. Prison, beatings, official floggings, stoning, shipwrecks: in the ancient world all these would mean not only that you were an unsavoury character whom most people rightly avoided, but that the gods must be angry with you as well. The dangers he faced and the hardships he endured were not the sort of thing that cultured and educated people, the great and the good, would put up with; they would have insisted on a military escort, or at least on travelling with people who could protect them. They wouldn't expect to have to go hungry, or cold, or without sleep; that would be very demeaning. Yet these are precisely the things that Paul boasts of.

The crunch of the whole passage is therefore verse 30: if I am forced to boast, I will boast of the things that show how weak I am. Paul has won, not the *corona muralis*, the 'crown of the wall', but the crown that really matters – the *corona Christi*, the 'crown of the **Messiah**'. His master was taken off in disgrace to die outside the city walls. The **apostle** was let down in a basket and ran away. Somehow the church in Corinth, and the church in the world of today, have to learn to stand normal cultural values on their head, to live the upside-down life, or rather the right-way-up **life**, of the true servants of the Messiah.

2 CORINTHIANS 12.1–10

The Vision and the Thorn

[1]I just have to boast – not that there's anything to be gained by it; but I'll go on to visions and revelations of the Lord. [2]Someone I know in the Messiah, fourteen years ago (whether in the body or out of the body I don't know, though God knows), was snatched up to the third heaven. [3]I know that this Someone person (whether in the body or apart from the body I don't know, God knows) – [4]this person was snatched up to Paradise, and heard . . . words you can't pronounce, which humans aren't allowed to repeat. [5]I will boast of Someone like that, but I won't boast of myself, except of my weaknesses. [6]If I did want to boast, you see, I wouldn't be mad; I'd be speaking the truth. But I'm holding back, so that nobody will think anything of me except what they can see in me or hear from me, [7]even considering how remarkable the revelations were.

As a result, so that I wouldn't become too exalted, a thorn was given to me in my flesh, a messenger from the satan, to keep stabbing away at me. [8]I prayed to the Lord three times about this, asking that it would be taken away from me, [9]and this is what he said to me: 'My grace is enough for you; my power comes to perfection in weakness.' So I will be all the more pleased to boast of my weaknesses, so that the Messiah's power may rest upon me. [10]So I'm delighted when I'm weak, insulted, in difficulties, persecuted and facing disasters, for the Messiah's sake. When I'm weak, you see, then I am strong.

Daedalus was a legendary Greek sculptor and craftsman, famous throughout the ancient world for his many clever inventions. It's probable that he really did exist, though many of the stories about him and his work are clearly made up after his time. Some said that the statues he carved could move all by themselves. But the thing for which he's most famous is flying.

Daedalus had gone to Crete, where he worked for the equally famous king Minos, and built for him the great labyrinth which comes into other ancient stories. But when he wanted to leave the island again, Minos wouldn't let him; so he applied his inventor's brain to the problem, and figured out a way to fly. He made wings out of birds' feathers, and attached them to his arms and shoulders with wax. He did the same for his son, Icarus. Off they flew, and were heading back to mainland Greece; but Icarus became too excited by this new form of travel, and wanted to fly, not onwards to their destination, but upwards towards the sun. Daedalus did his best to warn him that this would be dangerous, but the headstrong Icarus didn't listen. Then, sure enough, as he got closer to the sun, the heat began to melt the wax holding his wings in place. Off came the feathers, and Icarus fell into the sea and was drowned.

The story was often told in the ancient world, and often painted in the Renaissance period. The moral was obvious: don't fly too high, or you may come to a bad end. Don't be too proud, or presume too much on the strange things that can happen, or everything may go horribly wrong. This is a well-known moral lesson in many cultures.

What we find in this passage is the more particularly Christian version of the same point. Paul is speaking of the extraordinary and lavish spiritual experiences he has had, but in the same breath he speaks of his 'thorn in the flesh'. He couldn't simply enjoy living on a higher plane than everyone else; that might easily have made him too exalted. He might have become proud. He might have thought he could boast . . .

. . . Which is of course the point. This is the climax of his own 'boasting' list, which he has carefully constructed in such a way as to pull the rug out from under the 'boasting' which the rival teachers have been indulging in at Corinth. Not content with the teasing parody of standard social boasting in chapter 11, Paul now comes to the heart of the matter. The other teachers have placed great emphasis on spiritual experiences, on the wonderful things they have seen in visions and revelations, on the divine or angelic words they have heard. 'Ordinary' Christians would be in awe of them. Surely they must be super-spiritual, to have that kind of experience! Surely (they will have thought) such people must have been lifted beyond the condition of folk like ourselves! And so Paul takes it upon himself to show how even the most exalted spiritual experiences are to be understood within the framework of the **gospel**.

The teachers in Corinth would have told stories about themselves: I was transported to another realm, I heard this, I saw that, I met an angel. Paul refuses to do this – though it becomes clear by verse 7 that he is indeed talking about himself. He talks about Someone, someone he knows who is a member of the **Messiah**'s family.

The teachers would have liked what people today call an 'up-to-date testimony'. What has been happening in your spiritual life this last week? they might ask. Paul tells them a story about something that happened fourteen years ago. What, Paul, nothing more recent than that? No visions in the last few days?

The teachers would have been delighted to explain in great detail what had happened to them: whether they had been transported bodily to another place (like Ezekiel in the Old Testament), or whether this was some kind of out-of-the-body experience. Paul has no idea what was going on. He has no explanation. Enough to know that God knows.

The teachers would have been eager to come back with news of the wonderful words they had heard. What wisdom, what insight, what truth now to be revealed! Paul declares that this Someone person heard – but he's not allowed to say the words. Nobody is allowed to speak them.

By now the point is getting across. Visions and revelations do happen. Wonderful, uplifting, exalted spiritual states do occur. They are in a different league altogether from the states of mind and consciousness most of us experience most of the time. They can be real and magnificent gifts of God, marvellously encouraging, a real taste of paradise itself. But they are not given to people in order to make them special. To think like that is to fly too high, to forget that, in this life, the wings are always fastened on with wax.

A Roman general or emperor, parading through the throng of cheering crowds at a great triumphal procession, would have a slave in the chariot with him, whose job it was to whisper in his ear, 'Remember, you too are mortal.' The ancients recognized – mostly – that it was dangerous to become too elated; you could become guilty of what they called 'hubris', arrogant pride. Paul, too, has something that whispers like that in his ear: 'a thorn in my flesh'.

There has been endless speculation about what this was. A recurrent disease is the most likely guess, but we have no idea what sort. Or it might simply be the regular persecution which Paul always suffered, as he said in the previous chapter. But the point is not just that it happened, and niggled away at him so that he couldn't simply enjoy his wonderful spiritual experiences for their own sake. The point is that he prayed hard and long for God to take it away, *and God said 'No'*. That is the ultimate answer to the boasting of the Corinthian teachers.

You can feel their expectations building up as Paul tells the story of this satanic 'messenger' that has come to trouble him. Surely, Paul, the teachers would have said, it can't be God's will for you to suffer such a thing? Claim the victory of Jesus over the **satan**, and you'll get rid of it! Yes, says Paul, three times I prayed to the Lord about it . . . (and the Corinthians, listening, will be thinking: And on the third time the Lord took it away . . .) and God said – something quite different from what anyone had been expecting. Now at last Paul is allowed, it seems, to reveal a direct word that he has received from God, but it isn't a word that will let him or anyone else become puffed up in their own self-importance. Instead, it is one of the most comforting, reassuring, healing and steadying 'words of the Lord' ever recorded: 'My grace is enough for you; my power comes to perfection in weakness.' This is, after all, the same lesson he was trying to teach the Corinthians at the beginning of the first letter. In a sense, it is the underlying lesson he has been trying to teach them all through. 'When I am weak, then I am strong.' God's power and human power are not only not the same thing; often the second has to be knocked out of the way altogether for the first to shine through as God desires and intends.

Paul knew all about rich and varied spiritual experiences, visions and revelations. Just as he spoke in tongues more than all the Corinthians (1 Corinthians 14.18), but chose to speak ordinary human languages in church so that others would be built up in **faith**, so he has spiritual experiences of all sorts, but knows that the important point is not his spirituality – let alone any 'power' that that might give him – but God's grace. He has discovered that there is a different kind of strength, the kind that's really worth having, and that to possess it you have to be weak. And he's discovered that that is part of what the gospel of the crucified Messiah is all about.

2 CORINTHIANS 12.11–18

The Signs of a True Apostle

[11]I've been a fool! You forced me into it. If I *was* to have received an official commendation, it ought actually to have

come from you! After all, I'm not inferior to the super-apostles, even though I am nothing. [12]The signs of a true apostle, you see, were performed among you in all patience, with signs and wonders and powers. [13]In what way have you been worse off than all the other churches, except in the fact that I myself didn't become a burden to you? Forgive me this injustice!

[14]Now look: this is the third time I'm ready to come to you. And I'm not going to be a burden, because I'm not looking for what belongs to you, but you yourselves. It isn't children who ought to put things in store for their parents, you see; it's parents who ought to be storing things up for their children! [15]For my part, I will gladly spend and be spent on your behalf. If I love you all the more, am I going to be loved any the less?

[16]Grant me this, that I didn't lay any burden on you. But – maybe I was a trickster, and I took you by deceit! [17]Did I cheat you by any of the people I sent to you? [18]I urged Titus to go to you, and I sent the brother with him. Did Titus cheat you? He behaved in the same spirit as me, didn't he? He conducted himself in the same manner, didn't he?

All the time I have been writing this book, great events have been going on around me. A royal death, followed by the lying-in-state, the official mourning, and then the majestic and solemn funeral, have made the whole country pause and ask in a new way what monarchy is all about. The answer given by many commentators, often to their surprise, is that it's all about public service. It is about certain people being set aside from what they might otherwise have chosen to do with their lives, and commissioned – consecrated, in fact – to work tirelessly to hold together the nation, to build up its life, to establish and maintain justice and mercy, wisdom and truth, throughout the land.

Of course, critics of monarchy, even the constitutional variety, have always argued that these things are an illusion: that kings and queens rule for their own advantage, glorifying themselves in the process. But it need not be so, and it is by no means always so. Indeed, sometimes constitutional monarchs put to shame elected heads of state, not to mention prime ministers and government officials, whose attempts to bribe the electorate so that they can enjoy power are often far more self-seeking and self-serving than anything a contemporary Western monarch might do.

The debates about rulership, leadership, service and the dangers of self-seeking authority are at the centre of this letter, and Paul has now completed all the main things he wants to say about them. There remains the final exhortation, clearing the way for him to come at last for his third visit (the first one being when he founded the church, the second one being the 'painful visit' of 2.1). And he wants them to know that in coming to them the only thing he is seeking, the only reason he wants to come at all, is so that he can be their servant. He has no ambitions to be given great glory by them, still less money for his own enrichment. On the contrary: if anyone is going to be helping, strengthening and even enriching anyone else, it ought to be he, the **apostle** himself, who is coming to benefit the whole church. It is, after all, parents who save up in order to look after their children, not the other way around. And his deepest motivation for everything he does is his love for them, the love which has sought their welfare all along, and now drives Paul, despite all the agony of recent weeks, to come to them once more.

But of course, in claiming that he is the 'father' of the church, and that they are his 'children', he is making it clear once more that he has a unique relationship with them which no other teacher or leader can ever have. This makes it all the more ironic that he has been writing a letter like this, writing in effect his own 'letter of recommendation', even though it's been upside down and inside out. This has been a running theme from early on in the letter (3.1; 4.2; 5.12; 6.4; 10.12; 10.18). Indeed, it seems to have been one of the main reasons why Paul was writing at all, and why, in particular, he has written the sort of letter he has, heavy with irony and teasing, particularly in the section that has just concluded. He has been forced into 'boasting', though he has made sure he has boasted of all the wrong things: as though a queen, forced to produce a passport photograph to prove who she was, should deliberately produce an unflattering picture of herself taken by an amateur photographer.

What sort of 'recommendation', then, ought he to offer, and ought they to recognize? The answer is simple: the recommendation of the 'signs of an apostle'. These signs are not showy teaching styles, social status, and the kind of prestige that the rival teachers were striving for. They are the results of the preaching and living of the **gospel** of Jesus: the signs, wonders and powers that are seen when the **holy spirit** is truly at work. They should have given him this 'recommendation' themselves, since they knew that these things happened when he was with them at the beginning.

But the slanders and sneers of the newly arrived teachers had turned their minds away from Paul. In particular, they had allowed themselves to believe the suggestion that he didn't take money from them because he didn't love them – and then the suggestion, which clearly still rankles in Paul's mind, that he had been crafty, and had used his tactic of not receiving payment to win them over to his message. Once again, Paul finds himself condemned if he does this and condemned if he does that. That is how innuendo always works: when you want to besmirch someone's character, it's not difficult to twist anything they do or say and imply that their motives are not to be trusted. Ask any journalist.

Paul defends himself stoutly, and not only himself but his companions as well. Titus and the (still unnamed) fellow Christian who went with him have also behaved irreproachably. They know that; so why are they listening to lies?

The underlying lesson which emerges from this passage is a hard one for churches to learn. Perhaps that's why 2 Corinthians, except for certain selected highlights from earlier on in the letter, is not so often taken as a text for Bible study courses or sermons. It is that true gospel ministry, truly apostolic work, is powerful and effective – but will almost certainly be misunderstood and attacked, including by those who ought to know better. Whatever a humble, wise and godly Christian leader does, he or she can be certain of angry letters, abuse and personal attacks. That is how it has been from the beginning. We must not ignore the armoury of tricks that the **satan** has at his disposal (2.11).

And the proper way of handling such attacks is neither to respond in kind nor to protect oneself by erecting a wall of steel. Paul remains deeply vulnerable throughout this whole process, and has responded to attack with patient argument, biblical exposition, explanation of circumstances, direct personal appeal, and a fair amount of humour and irony. Only occasionally has he spoken directly about the people who are deliberately making trouble and attacking him, and then his words, though sharp, have themselves been thoroughly explicable in terms of the situation. If the church had carefully studied not only the Pauline gospel but how it works in the practice of apostolic ministry, a great deal of heartache might have been avoided in later generations.

2 CORINTHIANS 12.19—13.4

What Will Happen When Paul Arrives?

[19]You will imagine we are explaining ourselves again. Well, we're speaking in God's presence, in the Messiah! My beloved ones, it has all been intended to build you up. [20]I'm afraid, you see, that when I come I may find you rather different from what I would wish – and *I* may turn out to be rather different

137

from what *you* would wish! I'm afraid there may still be fighting, jealousy, anger, selfishness, slander, gossip, arrogance and disorder. [21]I'm afraid that perhaps, when I come once more, my God may humble me again in front of you, and I will have to go into mourning over many who sinned before, and have not repented of the uncleanness and fornication and shameless immorality that they have practised.

[13.1]This is the third time I'm coming to you. 'Every charge must be substantiated at the mouth of two or three witnesses.' [2]I said it before when I was with you the second time, and I say it now in advance while I'm away from you, to all those who had sinned previously, and all the others, that when I come back again I won't spare them – [3]since you are looking for proof of the Messiah who speaks in me, the Messiah who is not weak towards you but powerful in your midst! [4]He was crucified in weakness, you see, but he lives by God's power. For we too are weak in him, but we shall live with him, for your benefit, by God's power.

Three of the letters in the New Testament – the two letters addressed to Timothy, and the one to Titus – are known as 'The Pastoral Epistles'. But actually, the more I read our present letter, 2 Corinthians, the more I think that this is the supreme 'pastoral epistle' of the New Testament, perhaps of all time. It is hard enough to be a pastor when you're there with the congregation day after day, and can look them in the eye, sense their mood, discuss problems with them as they arise, and above all worship and pray with them daily and weekly and all round the year. There are still enormous problems which arise, for any pastor, preacher, priest or bishop. How much more difficult is it when you're doing your pastoral work, of necessity, at one remove, and through letters, knowing that there are people in the community who are working systematically to undermine you. This letter has the sure touch of someone who prays for his people, loves them unreservedly, and remains personally open to them, involved with them, vulnerable before them. It is a deeply risky position to be in.

And yet Paul persists. The two paragraphs here balance one another delicately, leaving us wondering what he really thought was going to happen, and how he would deal with it.

From earlier in the letter, we might have thought that all the problems had been dealt with. Chapters 2 and 7 suggest as much. Some have even taken this as an indication that different sections of the letter were written at different times, and that what we now print as chapters 10 to 13, or parts of them, were originally written and sent earlier than the rest. Perhaps, some have said, they formed the 'painful letter' of 2.4. But I don't think this is necessary. Chapters 10 to 13, though stern at one level, have as we have seen a teasing quality, poking fun at the rival teachers as much as warning against them. I think they are simply realistic. Paul knew enough about human nature, and about church life, to know that when people say very firmly one day that they are now completely decided, they've made up their minds, and that from this moment on everything is going to be different, the strong probability is that some of them, before the week is out, will have gone back on their word and returned to the old patterns of behaviour.

So my guess is that the anxiety he expresses here, in 12.20 and 21, is not a sign that something has happened to make him think differently from what he said in 7.5–16. At one level Paul does indeed have complete confidence in them, in (that is) the church as a whole. They have said they are right behind him and are looking forward to his arrival, and he isn't questioning that. But, as every pastor knows, there may well be some within the congregation who have not disagreed with what the majority have said, but who are privately still cherishing all kinds of things they ought to have abandoned long ago. The sins that form the ugly catalogue in verse 20 are all things that threaten the very life of a community. If anyone supposes

139

that, because the church as a whole has declared its loyalty to its true leaders, these sins will disappear overnight, I can only assume that they are living on a different planet from the one I know. Likewise, the sexual sins mentioned in verse 21 are capable of getting a hold on those who commit them at a very deep level. However much they may say, and mean it, that they have repented of them once and for all, there is always a real danger that they will go back on their word.

So what is Paul going to do about it? What does he mean when he says he won't spare those who persist in sins, whether of the jealousy-and-gossip variety or the sexual sort? We can only guess, but my guess is that, as in 1 Corinthians 5, he would cause such people to be excluded from the church and its fellowship, not least from the Lord's supper. This would require, of course, the consent and co-operation of most of the church, but Paul believes he can count on that; hence his quotation (in 13.1) of the rule in Deuteronomy about accusations needing to be supported by at least two witnesses. He envisages the possibility that he will have to sit as a judge, hearing accusations against church members and deciding, under God, what course of action is best to take against those who are found guilty. And, since there is never a suggestion in the early church that discipline took any other form, the main option seems to be expulsion, whether temporary or permanent.

Paul will come to them, then, in a strange mixture of weakness and power. He has made himself extremely vulnerable in this letter, laying himself open no doubt to all kinds of fresh possibilities of misunderstanding. His ironic 'boasting' in chapter 11 could backfire horribly, though the fact that he has dared to write such a spectacular passage is a fair indication that he believed it wouldn't. His description of his own near-despair in chapter 1 could easily be quoted against him: what was he doing, an **apostle** of the **Messiah**, feeling like that? But the **gospel** continues to undergird all his thinking, all his planning. The Messiah was crucified in weakness, but he lives by God's power! That is the basis for everything he does; that's why he can say that his own strange blend of radical weakness and spiritual power are the sure sign that the Messiah is indeed at work in him, and speaking through him (13.3 – another indication of the remarkable challenge that the rival teachers had posed).

My impression today is that pastors still find it difficult to maintain the balance. Some take their office and responsibility so seriously that they exercise an almost tyrannical rule over their people, insisting on getting their own way about everything and making life very uncomfortable for any who disagree. Others are so anxious not to be seen in that way that they never dare to warn people about the consequences of wicked behaviour, never exercise any discipline at all, and never lead. Somehow the combination of weakness and strength which we see in the gospel must enrich and inform all our pastoral work. Often it is only the wounded who can heal. Often it is only those who have themselves received the sentence of death (1.9) who can sit as judges. And if judgment of any sort still sounds peculiar (someone is bound to say 'how very unchristian!'), ask yourself which New Testament you're reading.

2 CORINTHIANS 13.5–10

Test Yourselves!

⁵Test yourselves to see if you really are in the faith! Put yourselves through the examination. Or don't you realize that Jesus the Messiah is in you? – unless, that is, you've failed the test. ⁶I hope you will discover that we didn't fail the test. ⁷But we pray to God that you will never, ever do anything wrong; not so that we can be shown up as having passed the test, but so that you will do what is right, even if that means that we appear like

people who've failed. [8]For we cannot do anything against the truth, but only for the truth. [9]We celebrate, you see, when we are weak but you are strong.

This is what we pray for, that you may become complete and mature. [10]That's why I'm writing this to you while I'm away, so that when I come I won't have to use my authority to be severe with you. The Lord has given me this authority, after all, not to pull down but to build up.

These days all sorts of machines come with their own inbuilt self-test system. My computer printer will run a self-test automatically if there has been some malfunction or error. Some modern cars have components that will check, all by themselves, to make sure that things are functioning properly. We all want things to work efficiently, but manufacturers know that if they leave things to us, to check and test the machines, we may forget, or do it wrong. Better to build the self-test capability into the machine itself.

Of course, there has been something of a craze for human self-testing as well, at least at a popular level. Magazine articles regularly invite you to work through a list of questions, with a range of possible answers, and then to add up your score and discover whether you're a good spouse, or a caring employer, or maybe whether you're likely to have a heart attack. Most of us do these from time to time and then quickly forget the result – though perhaps if you discovered you were at high risk of medical emergency, the self-test might prompt you to visit your doctor.

The Corinthians had been asking Paul for proof that the **Messiah** really was living and speaking in and through him (13.3). Paul has assured them that plenty of proof will be forthcoming if they are so bold as to challenge him in person. But now he turns the tables on them and suggests that they, too, should submit to a self-test. Before he arrives, they would be well advised to run through a checklist of the signs that indicate whether the Messiah's **life**, his crucified and risen life, is present. For Paul, that is the very centre of what it means to be a Christian (see Romans 8.9–10 and Galatians 2.20). When you look at yourself in the mirror, do you see someone in whom King Jesus is living and active, or someone who once knew him but now seems not to? When you listen to the sort of things you yourself say, does it sound like words that might have come from King Jesus himself, or are you simply talking the same way everyone else does? When you find yourself with your brother and sister Christians, do you respond to them as brothers and sisters, as people in whom you see King Jesus also living, or are they just 'other people'? And when you settle down and quieten your mind and heart, to pray and wait for God, do you know and sense the presence, the life and the love of King Jesus close to you, within you, warming and sustaining, guarding and guiding, checking and directing you?

These are searching tests, but they are the kind of thing Paul has in mind. And he longs to find that they have passed the test. In fact, he longs for this so much that he declares, as he does on one or two other occasions (like Romans 9.3), that he would rather *he* failed the test and they passed it than that he would pass it and they would all fail (verse 7). It wouldn't say much about his apostleship, after all, if he turned out to be a genuine Christian and all the people in a church he'd founded turned out to be fakes. He has no interest, any more than he has had throughout the letter, in proving himself to be someone extra special. He is simply an **apostle** of the crucified and risen Messiah – though that of course is quite special enough. It isn't a matter of his wanting to demonstrate his own status over against theirs, as though they were in a lawsuit one against the other. He is only interested in working for the truth (verse 8). If that means that he will appear weak and they strong, so be it (verse 9; compare 4.12).

What he wants above all is for the church to grow to full

maturity (verse 9). The word he uses, though, doesn't just mean 'mature' in the sense of a human being growing up, or a tree getting to the point where it can bear fruit. If Paul had had machines anything like the ones we know, this is the word he would have used to describe what happens when a machine is put into proper running order, when all its parts are functioning properly in themselves and working in harmony with each other. That is what he longs to see in Corinth, and that's what he's praying for in particular.

It's also why he's writing this letter. He wants to be able to use for its proper purpose the authority which the Lord has given him. Paul quotes a famous passage from the prophet Jeremiah (24.6), which he's already referred to earlier in the letter (10.8). Paul may well have identified with Jeremiah in various ways. When he describes his own call to be an apostle (Galatians 1.15), there are echoes of Jeremiah's call (1.5); Jeremiah's original commission was both 'to pluck up and break down' and 'to build and plant' (1.10). But in Jeremiah 24 God promises the exiles in Babylon that he will bring them back to their own land, and will build them up and not pull them down, plant them and not pluck them up – a promise reaffirmed twice, in the famous 'new **covenant**' passage (Jeremiah 31.28) and then again in 42.10. Paul's whole argument in the earlier part of the letter was that God had qualified and equipped him to bring this 'new covenant' into effect, bringing God's people back from the **exile** of sin and death and building them up into the mature, complete people of God in the Messiah. So his ambition for the church in Corinth is directly related to his perception of himself, his calling, and the prophetic roots of his work. What God promised in the Bible long ago is now at last coming true – or it will, if only the Corinthians and others learn to let the life of the Messiah have full value within them.

This is another hugely challenging passage for anyone who

wants to take the Christian faith seriously – and also for anyone called to Christian ministry. There is such a thing as a God-given authority in ministry, but its proper use is for building the community up, not for pulling it down. If something in the building is seriously wrong, the same authority can and must be used to put it right, pulling down whatever is in the wrong place. But the work of the **gospel**, of the strength which comes through weakness, is not primarily about that sort of activity. It is about the new covenant between the one God and his worldwide people being established, as communities learn what it means to have the life of the Messiah living within them.

Test yourselves, then . . .

2 CORINTHIANS 13.11–13

Grace, Love and Fellowship

[11]All that remains, my dear family, is this: celebrate, put everything in order, strengthen one another, think in the same way, be at peace; and the God of love and peace will be with you. [12]Greet one another with the holy kiss. All God's people send you their greetings.

[13]The grace of the Lord, King Jesus, the love of God, and the fellowship of the holy spirit be with you all.

The final sentence of 2 Corinthians is one of the most famous lines anywhere in Paul – so famous, in fact, that many people who hear it, or say it regularly, don't even realize it *is* by Paul, and wouldn't be able to find it if they thought it was. It's become a regular prayer, or blessing, in many churches and Christian groups. It sums up so much of what being a Christian is all about; it draws the focus firmly on to the God we know in and through Jesus and the **spirit**; and it takes the rich practical meaning and the rich theological meaning and turns them together into an elegant prayer. No wonder it has become so popular.

It's worth pausing on this verse and digging a little deeper, before we let the familiar words wash over us and forget what they actually mean. Let's begin with what they say about being a Christian.

Being a Christian starts, of course, with *grace*. The reason we are what we are at all is because the living God has reached down to us in sheer undeserved mercy. That's what Paul celebrates in his **gospel**, again and again. But we've also seen, not least in chapter 8 of this letter, that Paul can also use the word 'grace' to describe not only what God freely and lovingly does *for* us, but also what he does *in* us and also *through* us; more particularly, to describe what God did in and through the churches in Macedonia when he stirred them up to give generously, even beyond their means. There is solid sense to this second meaning, because the primary thing 'grace' referred to was the totally generous and self-giving love of God. We shouldn't be surprised if those whose lives are transformed by grace become, in turn, generous and self-giving people.

So why does Paul speak of the grace of *Jesus*, the King, the Lord, rather than simply of God? Well, that's what he spoke about in 8.9: in urging the Corinthians to give generously, he used the example of Jesus himself, leaving the riches of his heavenly existence and choosing to become poor and humble on our behalf. We could put it like this: Jesus is the person the generous and self-giving God became. Jesus *embodied* the grace of God. In Jesus grace became human, because that's what grace needed to do to be fully itself, to give itself for the world. We can properly speak, therefore, of 'the grace of the Lord, King Jesus', and we can pray, as Paul does here, that this grace will be powerfully active in the life of the church. That sums up one entire train of thought in this letter.

But behind and around this specific active power is 'the love of God'. In the New Testament, God's love is not simply one aspect of his character; it is the very heart, the essence of who God is. Love is, of course, a deeply personal quality, perhaps we should say the highest personal quality there is. And it is noticeable that the Jewish and Christian declaration of belief in a God of love as the only true God stands out a mile from most other views of God ancient or modern. The ancient pagan world certainly didn't believe in a God of love. Some of the gods and goddesses might show love, of a kind, for certain people, but that world was full of the anxiety that comes from a fear of superhuman forces that are precisely not loving, but are instead capricious, malevolent, and needing to be pacified or placated. None of the multiple options in that most pluralist of religious worlds spoke of a single God whose innermost nature was love.

This is hardly surprising, because the experience of life that most people have is hardly one of unmixed happiness; and, if there is one God who made the world, most people who think at all about the world will conclude that this God can hardly be loving. But what Judaism clung to as hope, and what Christianity announced as fulfilled at last, was the belief that the one God who made the world *was* indeed a totally loving God, who would demonstrate this love by acting within the world, at enormous cost to himself, to put everything right at last. And in gazing upon that loving God, and learning to trust and love him in return, the early Christians found themselves embraced in a new kind of spirituality, an intimacy of trust like that of children with a father, a warm security of knowing that they were loved with an everlasting love. That is what Paul means by 'the love of God'.

But those who are grasped by this love, who have the grace of the Lord Jesus in their bloodstreams, are thereby joined together in a family which the world has never seen before. It is a family not at all based on physical or ethnic descent or relation; anyone and everyone is welcome in it, which was just as challenging to most ancient people as it is to most modern ones. It is a family called to share a common life, and the word Paul uses here, *koinonia*, can be translated 'partnership', 'association', 'participation', 'sharing', 'communion', or even 'interchange', as well as the familiar 'fellowship'. This *koinonia* has been under enormous strain as Paul and the Corinthians have struggled to work out their relationship through visits, letters, reports, rumours, sorrow, joy, despair and hope. It is because Paul believes passionately that God's own spirit is at work in both his life and that of the Corinthians that he cannot let them go, cannot walk away and found another church somewhere else, cannot simply bask in the happy relationship he enjoys with his beloved Macedonian churches, but must thrash things out, must let partnership, participation and fellowship have their full expression. Indeed, if you want to know what 'the fellowship of the **holy spirit**' means in practice, a slow and serious reading of 2 Corinthians is a good, if sobering, place to start.

Each aspect of this threefold life, then, has been seen in the letter which is now drawing to a close. But Paul has not just provided a neat shorthand summary of the Christian life, the life in which he and the Corinthians share. He has provided an astonishingly brief yet complete picture of the God in whom Christians believe. Though he uses the word 'God' here as one of the three, his understanding of Jesus and the spirit elsewhere in his letters (and indeed the way in which, in this phrase, the three come so naturally together as the *source* of the blessings) forces us to see the whole phrase as describing the one God whom the earliest church came to see in threefold form. It would be over a century before theologians, greatly daring, began to use words like 'trinity' as a shorthand way of expressing what Paul is already articulating. But if such shorthand expressions hadn't been coined, it would be necessary for us to invent them if we were ever going to understand what Paul was getting at.

This has been controversial. Coming to know the one true God in and through Jesus of Nazareth, the crucified and risen one, and coming to know this God, and this Jesus, in and through the power and presence of the holy spirit, demands a change of heart, life, community and behaviour so thorough and costly that many back away from it. Indeed, the apparently simple instructions Paul gives to the church in verses 11 and 12 are themselves very demanding. The mutual greetings of peace might be quite an effort for some in the Corinthian church. But Paul leaves them, and us, with no choice. The God who said 'let light shine out of darkness' – the God, in other words, of both creation and new creation, of **covenant** and new covenant – has shone his brilliant light in our hearts, giving the light of the knowledge of the glory of God in the face of Jesus the King (4.6). Once that light has begun to illuminate the world around you, enabling you to see everything and everyone in a new way (5.16), the choice is clear. Either you must go forwards, at great cost, into that grace, love and fellowship; or you must step back into the darkness. Paul wrote this, his most deeply personal and heartfelt letter, to urge the Corinthians to do the former. He would wish no less for us.

GLOSSARY

accuser, *see* **the satan**

age to come, *see* **present age**

apostle, disciple, the Twelve

'Apostle' means 'one who is sent'. It could be used of an ambassador or official delegate. In the New Testament it is sometimes used specifically of Jesus' inner circle of twelve; but Paul sees not only himself but several others outside the Twelve as 'apostles', the criterion being whether the person had personally seen the risen Jesus. Jesus' own choice of twelve close associates symbolized his plan to renew God's people, Israel; after the death of Judas Iscariot (Matthew 27.5; Acts 1.18) Matthias was chosen by lot to take his place, preserving the symbolic meaning. During Jesus' lifetime they, and many other followers, were seen as his 'disciples', which means 'pupils' or 'apprentices'.

baptism

Literally, 'plunging' people into water. From within a wider Jewish tradition of ritual washings and bathings, **John the Baptist** undertook a vocation of baptizing people in the Jordan, not as one ritual among others but as a unique moment of **repentance**, preparing them for the coming of the **kingdom of God**. Jesus himself was baptized by John, identifying himself with this renewal movement and developing it in his own way. His followers in turn baptized others. After his **resurrection**, and the sending of the **holy spirit**, baptism became the normal sign and means of entry into the community of Jesus' people. As early as Paul it was aligned both with the **Exodus** from Egypt (1 Corinthians 10.2) and with Jesus' death and resurrection (Romans 6.2–11).

Christ, *see* Messiah

circumcision, circumcised

The cutting off of the foreskin. Male circumcision was a major mark of identity for Jews, following its initial commandment to Abraham (Genesis 17), reinforced by Joshua (Joshua 5.2–9). Other peoples, e.g. the Egyptians, also circumcised male children. A line of thought from Deuteronomy (e.g. 30.6), through Jeremiah (e.g. 31.33), to the **Dead Sea Scrolls** and the New Testament (e.g. Romans 2.29) speaks of 'circumcision of the heart' as God's real desire, by which one may become inwardly what the male Jew is outwardly, that is, marked out as part of God's people. At periods of Jewish assimilation into the surrounding culture, some Jews tried to remove the marks of circumcision (e.g. 1 Maccabees 1.11–15).

covenant

At the heart of Jewish belief is the conviction that the one God, YHWH, who had made the whole world, had called Abraham and his family to belong to him in a special way. The promises God made to Abraham and his family, and the requirements that were laid on them as a result, came to be seen in terms either of the agreement that a king would make with a subject people, or sometimes of the marriage bond between husband and wife. One regular way of describing this relationship was 'covenant', which can thus include both promise and **law**. The covenant was renewed at Mount Sinai with the giving of the **Torah**; in Deuteronomy before the entry to the promised land; and, in a more focused way, with David (e.g. Psalm 89). Jeremiah 31 promised that after the punishment of **exile** God would make a 'new covenant' with his people, forgiving them and binding them to him more intimately. Jesus believed that this was coming true through his **kingdom** proclamation and his death and **resurrection**. The early Christians developed these ideas in various ways, believing that in Jesus the promises had at last been fulfilled.

Dead Sea Scrolls

A collection of texts, some in remarkably good repair, some extremely fragmentary, found in the late 1940s around Qumran (near the northeast corner of the Dead Sea), and virtually all now edited, translated and in the public domain. They formed all or part of the library of a strict monastic group, most likely Essenes, founded in the mid-second century BC and lasting until the Jewish–Roman war of 66–70. The scrolls include the earliest existing manuscripts of the Hebrew and Aramaic scriptures, and several other important documents of community regulations, scriptural exegesis, hymns, wisdom writings, and other literature. They shed a flood of light on one small segment within the Judaism of Jesus' day, helping us to understand how some Jews at least were thinking, praying and reading scripture. Despite attempts to prove the contrary, they make no reference to **John the Baptist**, Jesus, Paul, James or early Christianity in general.

Essenes, *see* Dead Sea Scrolls

eucharist

The meal in which the earliest Christians, and Christians ever since, obeyed Jesus' command to 'do this in remembrance of him' at the Last Supper (Luke 22.19; 1 Corinthians 11.23–26). The word 'eucharist' itself comes from the Greek for 'thanksgiving'; it means, basically, 'the thank-you meal', and looks back to the many times when Jesus took bread, gave thanks for it, broke it, and gave it to people (e.g. Luke 24.30; John 6.11). Other early phrases for the same meal are 'the Lord's supper' (1 Corinthians 11.20) and 'the breaking of bread' (Acts 2.42). Later it came to be called 'the Mass' (from the Latin word at the end of the service, meaning 'sent out') and 'Holy Communion' (Paul speaks of 'sharing' or 'communion' in the body and blood of Christ). Later theological controversies about the precise meaning of the various actions and elements of the meal should not obscure its centrality in earliest Christian living and its continuing vital importance today.

exile

Deuteronomy (29—30) warned that if Israel disobeyed YHWH, he would send his people into exile, but that if they then repented he would bring them back. When the Babylonians sacked Jerusalem and took the people into exile, prophets such as Jeremiah interpreted this as the fulfilment of this prophecy, and made further promises about how long exile would last (70 years, according to Jeremiah 25.12; 29.10). Sure enough, exiles began to return in the late sixth century (Ezra 1.1).

However, the post-exilic period was largely a disappointment, since the people were still enslaved to foreigners (Nehemiah 9.36); and at the height of persecution by the Syrians, Daniel 9.2, 24 spoke of the 'real' exile lasting not for 70 years but for 70 *weeks* of years, i.e., 490 years. Longing for the real 'return from exile', when the prophecies of Isaiah, Jeremiah, etc. would be fulfilled, and redemption from pagan oppression accomplished, continued to characterize many Jewish movements, and was a major theme in Jesus' proclamation and his summons to **repentance**.

Exodus

The Exodus from Egypt took place, according to the book of that name, under the leadership of Moses, after long years in which the Israelites had been enslaved there. (According to Genesis 15.13f., this was itself part of God's covenanted promise to Abraham.) It demonstrated, to them and to Pharaoh, King of Egypt, that Israel was God's special child (Exodus 4.22). They then wandered through the Sinai wilderness for 40 years, led by God in a pillar of cloud and fire; early on in this time they were given the **Torah** on Mount Sinai itself. Finally, after the death of Moses and under the leadership of Joshua, they crossed the Jordan and entered, and eventually conquered, the promised land of Canaan. This event, commemorated annually in Passover and other Jewish festivals, gave the Israelites not only a powerful memory of what had made them a people, but also a particular shape and content to their faith in YHWH as not only creator but also redeemer; and in subsequent enslavements, particularly the **exile**, they looked for a further redemption which would be, in effect, a new Exodus. Probably no other past event so dominated the imagination of first-century Jews; among them the early Christians, following the lead of Jesus himself, continually referred back to the Exodus to give meaning and shape to their own critical events, most particularly Jesus' death and **resurrection**.

faith

Faith in the New Testament covers a wide area of human trust and trustworthiness, merging into love at one end of the scale and loyalty at the other. Within Jewish and Christian thinking faith in God also includes *belief*, accepting certain things as true about God, and what he has done in the world (e.g. bringing Israel out of Egypt; raising Jesus from the dead). For Jesus, 'faith' often seems to mean 'recognizing that God is decisively at work to bring the **kingdom** through Jesus'. For Paul, 'faith' is both the specific belief that Jesus is Lord and that God raised him from the dead (Romans 10.9) and the response of grateful human love to sovereign divine love (Galatians 2.20). This faith is, for Paul, the solitary badge of membership in God's people in **Christ**, marking them out in a way that **Torah**, and the works it prescribes, can never do.

Gehenna, hell

Gehenna is, literally, the valley of Hinnom, on the south-west slopes of Jerusalem. From ancient times it was used as a garbage dump, smouldering with a continual fire. Already by the time of Jesus some Jews used it as an image for the place of punishment after death. Jesus' own usage blends the two meanings in his warnings both to Jerusalem itself (unless it repents, the whole city will become a smouldering heap of garbage) and to people in general (to beware of God's final judgment).

Gentiles

The Jews divided the world into Jews and non-Jews. The Hebrew word for non-Jews, *goyim*, carries overtones both of family identity (i.e., not of Jewish ancestry) and of worship (i.e. of idols, not of the one true God YHWH). Though many Jews established good relations with Gentiles, not least in the Jewish Diaspora (the dispersion of Jews away from Palestine), officially there were taboos against contact such as intermarriage. In the New Testament the Greek word *ethne*, 'nations', carries the same meanings as *goyim*. Part of Paul's overmastering agenda was to insist that Gentiles who believed in Jesus had full rights in the Christian community alongside believing Jews, without having to become **circumcised**.

good news, gospel, message, word

The idea of 'good news', for which an older English word is 'gospel', had two principal meanings for first-century Jews. First, with roots in Isaiah, it meant the news of YHWH's long-awaited victory over evil and rescue of his people. Second, it was used in the Roman world of the accession, or birthday, or the emperor. Since for Jesus and Paul the announcement of God's inbreaking **kingdom** was both the fulfilment of prophecy and a challenge to the world's present rulers, 'gospel' became an important shorthand for both the message of Jesus himself, and the apostolic message about him. Paul saw this message as itself the vehicle of God's saving power (Romans 1.16; 1 Thessalonians 2.13).

The four canonical 'gospels' tell the story of Jesus in such a way as to bring out both these aspects (unlike some other so-called 'gospels' circulated in the second and subsequent centuries, which tended both to cut off the scriptural and Jewish roots of Jesus' achievement and to inculcate a private spirituality rather than confrontation with the world's rulers). Since in Isaiah this creative, life-giving good news was seen as God's own powerful word (40.8; 55.11), the early Christians could use 'word' or 'message' as another shorthand for the basic Christian proclamation.

gospel, *see* **good news**

heaven

Heaven is God's dimension of the created order (Genesis 1.1; Psalm 115.16; Matthew 6.9), whereas 'earth' is the world of space, time and matter that we know. 'Heaven' thus sometimes stands, reverentially, for 'God' (as in Matthew's regular '**kingdom** of heaven'). Normally hidden from human sight, heaven is occasionally revealed or unveiled so that people can see God's dimension of ordinary life (e.g. 2 Kings 6.17; Revelation 1, 4—5). Heaven in the New Testament is thus not usually seen as the place where God's people go after death; at the end the New Jerusalem descends *from* heaven *to* earth, joining the two dimensions for ever. 'Entering the kingdom of heaven' does not mean 'going to heaven after death', but belonging in the present to the people who steer their earthly course by the standards and purposes of heaven (cf. the Lord's Prayer: 'on earth as in heaven', Matthew 6. 10) and who are assured of membership in the **age to come**.

hell, *see* **Gehenna**

high priest, *see* **priests**

holy spirit

In Genesis 1.2, the spirit is God's presence and power *within* creation, without God being identified with creation. The same spirit entered people, notably the prophets, enabling them to speak and act for God. At his **baptism** by **John the Baptist**, Jesus was specially equipped with the spirit, resulting in his remarkable public career (Acts 10.38). After his **resurrection**, his followers were themselves filled (Acts 2) by the same spirit, now identified as Jesus' own spirit: the creator God was acting afresh, remaking the world and them too. The spirit enabled them to live out a holiness which the **Torah** could not, producing 'fruit' in their lives, giving them 'gifts' with which to serve God, the world, and the church, and assuring them of future resurrection (Romans 8; Galatians 4—5; 1 Corinthians 12—14). From very early in Christianity (e.g. Galatians 4.1–7), the spirit became part of the new revolutionary definition of God himself: 'the one who sends the son and the spirit of the son'.

John (the Baptist)

Jesus' cousin on his mother's side, born a few months before Jesus; his father was a **priest**. He acted as a prophet, baptizing in the Jordan – dramatically re-enacting the **Exodus** from Egypt – to prepare people, by **repentance**, for God's coming judgment. He may have had some contact with the **Essenes**, though his eventual public message was different from theirs. Jesus' own vocation was decisively confirmed at his **baptism** by John. As part of John's message of the **kingdom**, he outspokenly criticized Herod Antipas for marrying his brother's wife. Herod had him imprisoned, and then beheaded him at his wife's request (Mark 6.14–29). Groups of John's disciples continued a separate existence, without merging into Christianity, for some time afterwards (e.g. Acts 19.1–7).

justification

God's declaration, from his position as judge of all the world, that someone is in the right, despite universal sin. This declaration will be made on the last day on the basis of an entire life (Romans 2.1–16), but is brought forward into the present on the basis of Jesus' achievement, because sin has been dealt with through his cross (Romans 3.21—4.25); the means of this present justification is simply **faith**.

This means, particularly, that Jews and **Gentiles** alike are full members of the family promised by God to Abraham (Galatians 3; Romans 4).

kingdom of God, kingdom of heaven

Best understood as the king*ship*, or sovereign and saving rule, of Israel's God YHWH, as celebrated in several psalms (e.g. 99.1) and prophecies (e.g. Daniel 6.26f.). Because YHWH was the creator God, when he finally became king in the way he intended this would involve setting the world to rights, and particularly rescuing Israel from its enemies. 'Kingdom of God' and various equivalents (e.g. 'No king but God!') became a revolutionary slogan around the time of Jesus. Jesus' own announcement of God's kingdom redefined these expectations around his own very different plan and vocation. His invitation to people to 'enter' the kingdom was a way of summoning them to allegiance to himself and his programme, seen as the start of God's long-awaited saving reign. For Jesus, the kingdom was coming not in a single move, but in stages, of which his own public career was one, his death and **resurrection** another, and a still future consummation another. Note that 'kingdom of **heaven**' is Matthew's preferred form for the same phrase, following a regular Jewish practice of saying 'heaven' rather than 'God'. It does not refer to a place ('heaven'), but to the fact of God's becoming king in and through Jesus and his achievement. Paul speaks of Jesus, as **Messiah**, already in possession of his kingdom, waiting to hand it over finally to the father (1 Corinthians 15.23–28; cf. Ephesians 5.5).

law, *see* Torah

life, soul, spirit

Ancient people held many different views about what made human beings the special creatures they are. Some, including many Jews, believed that to be complete, humans needed bodies as well as inner selves. Others, including many influenced by the philosophy of Plato (fourth century BC), believed that the important part of a human was the 'soul' (Gk: *psyche*), which at death would be happily freed from its bodily prison. Confusingly for us, the same word *psyche* is often used in the New Testament within a Jewish framework where it clearly means 'life' or 'true self', without implying a body/soul dualism that devalues the body. Human inwardness of experience and understanding can also be referred to as 'spirit'. *See also* **resurrection**.

message, *see* **good news**

Messiah, messianic, Christ

The Hebrew word means literally 'anointed one', hence in theory either a prophet, **priest** or king. In Greek this translates as *Christos*; 'Christ' in early Christianity was a title, and only gradually became an alternative proper name for Jesus. In practice 'Messiah' is mostly restricted to the notion, which took various forms in ancient Judaism, of the coming king who would be David's true heir, through whom YHWH would bring judgment to the world, and in particular would rescue Israel from pagan enemies. There was no single template of expectations. Scriptural stories and promises contributed to different ideals and movements, often focused on (a) decisive military defeat of Israel's enemies and (b) rebuilding or cleansing the **Temple**. The **Dead Sea Scrolls** speak of two 'Messiahs', one a priest and the other a king. The universal early Christian belief that Jesus was Messiah is only explicable, granted his crucifixion by the Romans (which would have been seen as a clear sign that he was not the Messiah), by their belief that God had raised him from the dead, so vindicating the implicit messianic claims of his earlier ministry.

Mishnah

The main codification of Jewish law (**Torah**) by the **rabbis**, produced in about AD 200, reducing to writing the 'oral Torah' which in Jesus' day ran parallel to the 'written Torah'. The Mishnah is itself the basis of the much larger collections of traditions in the two Talmuds (roughly AD 400).

parousia

Literally, it means 'presence', as opposed to 'absence', and is sometimes used by Paul with this sense (e.g. Philippians 2.12). It was already used in the Roman world for the ceremonial arrival of, for example, the emperor at a subject city or colony. Although the ascended Lord is not 'absent' from the church, when he 'appears' (Colossians 3.4; 1 John

3.2) in his 'second coming' this will be, in effect, an 'arrival' like that of the emperor, and Paul uses it thus in 1 Corinthians 15.23; 1 Thessalonians 2.19; etc. In the **gospels** it is found only in Matthew 24 (vv. 3, 27, 39).

Pharisees, legal experts, lawyers, rabbis

The Pharisees were an unofficial but powerful Jewish pressure group through most of the first centuries BC and AD. Largely lay-led, though including some **priests**, their aim was to purify Israel through intensified observance of the Jewish law (**Torah**), developing their own traditions about the precise meaning and application of scripture, their own patterns of prayer and other devotion, and their own calculations of the national hope. Though not all legal experts were Pharisees, most Pharisees were thus legal experts.

They effected a democratization of Israel's life, since for them the study and practice of Torah was equivalent to worshipping in the **Temple** – though they were adamant in pressing their own rules for the Temple liturgy on an unwilling (and often **Sadducean**) priesthood. This enabled them to survive AD 70 and, merging into the early rabbinic movement, to develop new ways forward. Politically they stood up for ancestral traditions, and were at the forefront of various movements of revolt against both pagan overlordship and compromised Jewish leaders. By Jesus' day there were two distinct schools, the stricter one of Shammai, more inclined towards armed revolt, and the more lenient one of Hillel, ready to live and let live.

Jesus' debates with the Pharisees are at least as much a matter of agenda and policy (Jesus strongly opposed their separatist nationalism) as about details of theology and piety. Saul of Tarsus was a fervent right-wing Pharisee, presumably a Shammaite, until his conversion.

After the disastrous war of AD 66–70, these schools of Hillel and Shammai continued bitter debate on appropriate policy. Following the further disaster of AD 135 (the failed Bar-Kochba revolt against Rome) their traditions were carried on by the rabbis who, though looking to the earlier Pharisees for inspiration, developed a Torah-piety in which personal holiness and purity took the place of political agendas.

present age, age to come, eternal life

By the time of Jesus many Jewish thinkers divided history into two periods: 'the present age' and 'the age to come' – the latter being the time when YHWH would at last act decisively to judge evil, to rescue Israel, and to create a new world of justice and peace. The early Christians believed that, though the full blessings of the coming age lay still in the future, it had already begun with Jesus, particularly with his death and **resurrection**, and that by **faith** and **baptism** they were able to enter it already. 'Eternal life' does not mean simply 'existence continuing without end', but 'the life of the age to come'.

priests, high priest

Aaron, the older brother of Moses, was appointed Israel's first high priest (Exodus 28—29), and in theory his descendants were Israel's priests thereafter. Other members of his tribe (Levi) were 'Levites', performing other liturgical duties but not sacrificing. Priests lived among the people all around the country, having a local teaching role (Leviticus 10.11; Malachi 2.7), and going to Jerusalem by rotation to perform the **Temple** liturgy (e.g. Luke 2.8).

David appointed Zadok (whose Aaronic ancestry is sometimes questioned) as high priest, and his family remained thereafter the senior priests in Jerusalem, probably the ancestors of the **Sadducees**. One explanation of the origins of the **Qumran** Essenes is that they were a dissident group who believed themselves to be the rightful chief priests.

Qumran, *see* Dead Sea Scrolls

rabbis, *see* Pharisees

repentance

Literally, this means 'turning back'. It is widely used in the Old Testament and subsequent Jewish literature to indicate both a personal turning away from sin and Israel's corporate turning away from idolatry and back to YHWH. Through both meanings, it is linked to the idea of 'return from **exile**'; if Israel is to 'return' in all senses, it must 'return' to YHWH. This is at the heart of the summons of both **John the Baptist** and Jesus. In Paul's writings it is mostly used for **Gentiles** turning away from idols to serve the true God; also for sinning Christians who need to return to Jesus.

160

resurrection

In most biblical thought, human bodies matter and are not merely disposable prisons for the **soul**. When ancient Israelites wrestled with the goodness and justice of YHWH, the creator, they ultimately came to insist that he must raise the dead (Isaiah 26.19; Daniel 12.2–3) – a suggestion firmly resisted by classical pagan thought. The longed-for return from **exile** was also spoken of in terms of YHWH raising dry bones to new **life** (Ezekiel 37.1–14). These ideas were developed in the second-**Temple** period, not least at times of martyrdom (e.g. 2 Maccabees 7). Resurrection was not just 'life after death', but a newly embodied life *after* 'life after death'; those at present dead were either 'asleep', or seen as 'souls', 'angels' or 'spirits', awaiting new embodiment.

The early Christian belief that Jesus had been raised from the dead was not that he had 'gone to **heaven**', or that he had been 'exalted', or was 'divine'; they believed all those as well, but each could have been expressed without mention of resurrection. Only the bodily resurrection of Jesus explains the rise of the early church, particularly its belief in Jesus' messiahship (which his crucifixion would have called into question). The early Christians believed that they themselves would be raised to a new, transformed bodily life at the time of the Lord's return or **parousia** (e.g. Philippians 3.20f.).

sacrifice

Like all ancient people, the Israelites offered animal and vegetable sacrifices to their God. Unlike others, they possessed a highly detailed written code (mostly in Leviticus) for what to offer and how to offer it; this in turn was developed in the **Mishnah** (*c.* AD 200). The Old Testament specifies that sacrifices can only be offered in the Jerusalem **Temple**; after this was destroyed in AD 70, sacrifices ceased, and Judaism developed further the idea, already present in some teachings, of prayer, fasting and almsgiving as alternative forms of sacrifice. The early Christians used the language of sacrifice in connection with such things as holiness, evangelism and the **eucharist**.

Sadducees

By Jesus' day, the Sadducees were the aristocracy of Judaism, possibly tracing their origins to the family of Zadok, David's **high priest**. Based in Jerusalem, and including most of the leading priestly families, they had their own traditions and attempted to resist the pressure of the **Pharisees** to conform to theirs. They claimed to rely only on the Pentateuch (the first five books of the Old Testament), and denied any doctrine of a future life, particularly of the **resurrection** and other ideas associated with it, presumably because of the encouragement such beliefs gave to revolutionary movements. No writings from the Sadducees have survived, unless the apocryphal book of Ben-Sirach ('Ecclesiasticus') comes from them. The Sadducees themselves did not survive the destruction of Jerusalem and the **Temple** in AD 70.

the satan, 'the accuser', demons

The Bible is never very precise about the identity of the figure known as 'the satan'. The Hebrew word means 'the accuser', and at times the satan seems to be a member of YHWH's heavenly council, with special responsibility as director of prosecutions (1 Chronicles 21.1; Job 1—2; Zechariah 3.1f.). However, it becomes identified variously with the serpent of the garden of Eden (Genesis 3.1–15) and with the rebellious daystar cast out of **heaven** (Isaiah 14.12–15), and was seen by many Jews as the quasi-personal source of evil standing behind both human wickedness and large-scale injustice, sometimes operating through semi-independent 'demons'. By Jesus' time various words were used to denote this figure, including Beelzebul/b (lit. 'Lord of the flies') and simply 'the evil one'; Jesus warned his followers against the deceits this figure could perpetrate. His opponents accused him of being in league with the satan, but the early Christians believed that Jesus in fact defeated it both in his own struggles with temptation (Matthew 4; Luke 4), his exorcisms of demons, and his death (1 Corinthians 2.8; Colossians 2.15). Final victory over this ultimate enemy is thus assured (Revelation 20), though the struggle can still be fierce for Christians (Ephesians 6.10–20).

son of God

Originally a title for Israel (Exodus 4.22) and the Davidic king (Psalm 2.7); also used of ancient angelic figures (Genesis 6.2). By the New Testament period it was already used as a **messianic** title, for example in the **Dead Sea Scrolls**. There, and when used of Jesus in the **gospels** (e.g. Matthew 16.16), it means, or reinforces, 'Messiah', without the later significance of 'divine'. However, already in Paul the transition to the fuller meaning (one who was already equal with God and was sent by him to become human and to become Messiah) is apparent, without loss of the meaning 'Messiah' itself (e.g. Galatians 4.4).

son of man

In Hebrew or Aramaic, this simply means 'mortal' or 'human being'; in later Judaism, it is sometimes used to mean 'I' or 'someone like me'. In the New Testament the phrase is frequently linked to Daniel 7.13, where 'one like a son of man' is brought on the clouds of **heaven** to 'the Ancient of Days', being vindicated after a period of suffering, and is given kingly power. Though Daniel 7 itself interprets this as code for 'the people of the saints of the Most High', by the first century some Jews understood it as a **messianic** promise. Jesus developed this in his own way in certain key sayings which are best understood as promises that God would vindicate him, and judge those who had opposed him, after his own suffering (e.g. Mark 14.62). Jesus was thus able to use the phrase as a cryptic self-designation, hinting at his coming suffering, his vindication and his God-given authority.

soul, *see* life

spirit, *see* life, holy spirit

Temple

The Temple in Jerusalem was planned by David (*c*. 1000 BC) and built by his son Solomon as the central sanctuary for all Israel. After reforms under Hezekiah and Josiah in the seventh century BC, it was destroyed by Babylon in 587 BC. Rebuilding by the returned **exiles** began in 538 BC, and was completed in 516, initiating the 'second Temple period'. Judas Maccabaeus cleansed it in 164 BC after its desecration by Antiochus Epiphanes (167). Herod the Great began to rebuild and beautify it in 19 BC; the work was completed in AD 63. The Temple was destroyed by the Romans in AD 70. Many Jews believed it should and would be rebuilt; some still do. The Temple was not only the place of **sacrifice**; it was believed to be the unique dwelling of YHWH on earth, the place where **heaven** and earth met.

Torah, Jewish law

'Torah', narrowly conceived, consists of the first five books of the Old Testament, the 'five books of Moses' or 'Pentateuch'. (These contain much law, but also much narrative.) It can also be used for the whole Old Testament scriptures, though strictly these are the 'law, prophets and writings'. In a broader sense, it refers to the whole developing corpus of Jewish legal tradition, written and oral; the oral Torah was initially codified in the **Mishnah** around AD 200, with wider developments found in the two Talmuds, of Babylon and Jerusalem, codified around AD 400. Many Jews in the time of Jesus and Paul regarded the Torah as being so strongly God-given as to be almost itself, in some sense, divine; some (e.g. Ben Sirach 24) identified it with the figure of 'Wisdom'. Doing what Torah said was not seen as a means of earning God's favour, but rather of expressing gratitude, and as a key badge of Jewish identity.

word, *see* good news

Word

The prologue to John's gospel (1.1–18) uses Word (Greek: *logos*) in a special sense, based on the ancient Israelite view of God's Word in creation and new creation. Here the Word is Jesus, the personal presence of the God who remains other than the world. He is the one through whom creation came into being; he is the one, now, through whom it will be healed and restored.

YHWH

The ancient Israelite name for God, from at least the time of the **Exodus** (Exodus 6.2f.). It may originally have been pronounced 'Yahweh', but by the time of Jesus it was considered too holy to speak out loud, except for the **high priest** once a year in the Holy of Holies in the **Temple**. Instead, when reading scripture, pious Jews would say *Adonai*, 'Lord', marking this usage by adding the vowels of *Adonai* to the consonants of YHWH, eventually producing the hybrid 'Jehovah'. The word YHWH is formed from the verb 'to be', combining 'I am who I am', 'I will be who I will be', and perhaps 'I am because I am', emphasizing YHWH's sovereign creative power.